THE
DEITY OF
CHRIST

THE
DEITY OF
CHRIST

———⸎———

THE JOHN MACARTHUR STUDY SERIES

JOHN MACARTHUR

MOODY PUBLISHERS
CHICAGO

THE MASTER'S SEMINARY PRESS
LOS ANGELES

Unless otherwise indicated, Scripture quotations are from the New American Standard Bible®, Copyright © 1960, 1962, 1963, 1968, 1971, 1972, 1973, 1975, 1977, 1995 by The Lockman Foundation. Used by permission. (www.Lockman.org)

Scripture quotations marked KJV are taken from the King James Version.

Scripture quotations marked NKJV are taken from the New King James Version. Copyright © 1982 by Thomas Nelson. Used by permission. All rights reserved.

All websites listed herein are accurate at the time of publication but may change in the future or cease to exist. The listing of website references and resources does not imply publisher endorsement of the site's entire contents.

Edited by: Jim Vincent
Interior design: Ragont Design
Cover design: Erik M. Peterson
Cover image: Cover image of crown copyright © 2016 by Pearl / Lightstock (251520)

Library of Congress Cataloging-in-Publication Data

Names: MacArthur, John, 1939- author.
Title: The deity of Christ / John MacArthur.
Description: Chicago : Moody Publishers, 2017. | Series: The John MacArthur study series
Identifiers: LCCN 2016045245 (print) | LCCN 2016047111 (ebook) | ISBN 9780802415110 | ISBN 9780802495273
Subjects: LCSH: Jesus Christ--Divinity--Biblical teaching.
Classification: LCC BT216.3 .M33 2017 (print) | LCC BT216.3 (ebook) | DDC 232/.8--dc23
LC record available at https://lccn.loc.gov/2016045245

We hope you enjoy this book from Moody Publishers. Our goal is to provide high-quality, thought-provoking books and products that connect truth to your real needs and challenges. For more information on other books and products written and produced from a biblical perspective, go to www.moodypublishers.com or write to:

Moody Publishers
820 N. LaSalle Boulevard
Chicago, IL 60610

1 3 5 7 9 10 8 6 4 2

Printed in the United States of America

About This Series

This volume is part of *The John MacArthur Study Series*. It is comprised of chapters adapted from *The MacArthur New Testament Commentary*, which have been arranged thematically for the purpose of topical study. Accordingly, each chapter is designed to take the reader down deep into the text of Scripture, while the volume as a whole addresses a specific biblical theme.

This approach is ideal for anyone wanting to engage in an indepth study of what the Bible says about a given subject. It also serves as a valuable tool for pastors or Bible study leaders looking to teach a series on this important topic.

CONTENTS

PREFACE

No question is more important than "Who is Jesus Christ?" It is of ultimate significance because how people respond to the Lord Jesus determines their eternal destiny (John 3:36; cf. John 14:6; Acts 4:12). Those who wrongly answer that question will face divine judgment (cf. John 3:18; 1 Cor. 16:22; 1 John 4:3).

Throughout church history, many different answers have been offered in response to that critical question. False teachers (like the fourth-century heretic Arius and modern Jehovah's Witnesses) have suggested that Christ was merely a creature; while the ancient Gnostics taught that He was one of many divine entities. In the nineteenth-century, liberal theologians insisted Jesus was nothing more than a moral teacher and social activist who was misunderstood by the religious leaders. But those views, and others like them, fall woefully short of biblical truth.

The Word of God reveals that Jesus Christ was far more than a benevolent prophet or inspirational leader. In fact, He is infinitely more than any created being. As the author of Hebrews explains, the Lord Jesus "is the radiance of [the Father's] glory and the exact representation of His nature, and upholds all things by the word of His power" (Heb. 1:3). He is God incarnate, in whom "all the fullness of Deity dwells in bodily form" (Col. 2:9) and of whom the apostle John declared:

> In the beginning was the Word, and the Word was with God, and the Word was God. He was in the beginning with God. All things came into being through Him, and apart from Him nothing came into being that has come into being. . . . And the Word became flesh, and

dwelt among us, and we saw His glory, glory as of the only begotten from the Father, full of grace and truth. (John 1:1–3, 14)

Those passages are just the tip of the iceberg. The New Testament clearly and repeatedly emphasizes that Jesus Christ was no mere man. He is the eternal second member of the Trinity, the glorious Son of God who is worthy of our worship and obedience (Phil. 2:9–11).

There is great value in tracing a doctrine like the deity of Christ through the pages of Scripture. Because His deity is often attacked by cultic groups and skeptics, believers need to know what God's Word teaches about who Jesus truly is. Moreover, as their knowledge of the Savior deepens, their love for Him will only grow stronger.

My prayer for you, as you read this volume, is that the truth about "our great God and Savior, Christ Jesus" (Titus 2:13) will inform your mind, encourage your heart, fortify your will, ignite your worship, and motivate your obedience to Him.

John MacArthur

PART 1

THE DIVINE
GLORY OF CHRIST

Chapter 1

THE ETERNAL GLORY OF THE DIVINE WORD

JOHN 1:1–5

In the beginning was the Word, and the Word was with God, and the Word was God. He was in the beginning with God. All things came into being through Him, and apart from Him nothing came into being that has come into being. In Him was life, and the life was the Light of men. The Light shines in the darkness, and the darkness did not comprehend it. (1:1–5)

The opening section of John's gospel expresses the most profound truth in the universe in the clearest terms. Though the vocabulary is simple enough to be understood by a child, John's Spirit-inspired words convey a truth beyond the ability of the greatest minds in human history to fathom: the eternal, infinite God became a man in the Person of the Lord Jesus Christ. The glorious, incontrovertible truth that in Jesus the divine "Word became flesh" (1:14) is the theme of John's gospel.

The deity of the Lord Jesus Christ is an essential, nonnegotiable tenet of the Christian faith. Several lines of biblical evidence flow together to prove conclusively that He is God.

First, the direct statements of Scripture affirm that Jesus is God. In keeping with his emphasis on Christ's deity, John records several of those statements. The opening verse of his gospel declares, "The Word [Jesus] was God." In John's gospel Jesus repeatedly assumed for Himself the divine name, "I am" (cf. 4:26; 8:24, 28, 58; 13:19: 18:5, 6, 8). In 10:30, He claimed to be one in nature and essence with the Father (that the unbelieving Jews recognized this as a claim to deity is clear from their reaction in v. 33; cf. 5:18). Nor did Jesus correct Thomas when he addressed Him as "my Lord and my God!" (20:28); in fact, He praised the disciple for his faith (v. 29). Jesus' reaction is inexplicable if He were not God.

To the Philippians Paul wrote, "[Jesus] existed in the form of God," possessing absolute "equality with God" (Phil. 2:6). In Colossians 2:9 he declared, "For in Him all the fullness of Deity dwells in bodily form." Romans 9:5 refers to Christ as "God blessed forever"; Titus 2:13 and 2 Peter 1:1 call Him "our God and Savior." God the Father addressed the Son as God in Hebrews 1:8: "Your throne, O God, is forever and ever, and the righteous scepter is the scepter of His kingdom." In his first epistle John referred to Jesus Christ as "the true God" (1 John 5:20).

Second, Jesus Christ receives titles elsewhere in Scripture given to God. As noted above, Jesus took for Himself the divine name "I am." In John 12:40 John quoted Isaiah 6:10, a passage which in Isaiah's vision refers to God (cf. Isa. 6:5). Yet in verse 41 John declared, "These things Isaiah said because he saw His [Christ's; cf. vv. 36, 37, 42] glory, and he spoke of Him." Jeremiah prophesied that the Messiah would be called "The Lord [YHWH] our righteousness" (Jer. 23:6).

God and Jesus are both called Shepherd (Ps. 23:1 [God]— John 10:14 [Jesus]); Judge (Gen. 18:25—2 Tim. 4:1, 8); Holy One

(Isa. 10:20—Ps. 16:10; Acts 2:27; 3:14); First and Last (Isa. 44:6; 48:12—Rev. 1:17; 22:13); Light (Ps. 27:1—John 8:12); Lord of the Sabbath (Ex. 16:23, 29; Lev. 19:3—Matt. 12:8); Savior (Isa. 43:11—Acts 4:12; Titus 2:13); Pierced One (Zech. 12:10—John 19:37); Mighty God (Isa. 10:21—Isa. 9:6); Lord of Lords (Deut. 10:17—Rev. 17:14); and Redeemer (Isa. 41:14; 48:17; 63:16—Eph. 1:7; Heb. 9:12). In the final book of the Bible they both are called the Alpha and Omega (Rev. 1:8—Rev. 22:12-13), that is, the beginning and the end.

Third, Jesus Christ possesses the incommunicable attributes of God, those unique to Him. Scripture reveals Christ to be eternal (Mic. 5:2; Isa. 9:6), omnipresent (Matt. 18:20; 28:20), omniscient (Matt. 11:23; John 16:30; 21:17), omnipotent (Phil. 3:21), immutable (Heb. 13:8), sovereign (Matt. 28:18), and glorious (John 17:5; 1 Cor. 2:8; cf. Isa. 42:8; 48:11, where God states that He will not give His glory to another).

Fourth, Jesus Christ does the works that only God can do. He created all things (John 1:3; Col. 1:16), sustains the creation (Col. 1:17; Heb. 1:3), raises the dead (John 5:21; 11:25-44), forgives sin (Mark 2:10; cf. v. 7), and His word stands forever (Matt. 24:35; cf. Isa. 40:8).

Fifth, Jesus Christ receives worship (Matt. 14:33; 28:9; John 9:38; Phil. 2:10; Heb. 1:6)—even though He taught that only God is to be worshiped (Matt. 4:10). Scripture also records that both holy men (Acts 10:25-26) and holy angels (Rev. 22:8-9) refused worship.

Finally, Jesus Christ receives prayer, which is only to be addressed to God (John 14:13-14; Acts 7:59-60; 1 John 5:13-15).

Verses 1-18, the prologue to John's gospel, form a synopsis, or overview, of the entire book. John clearly defines his purpose in writing his gospel in 20:31—that his readers "may believe that Jesus is the Christ, the Son of God; and that believing [they] may have life in His name." John revealed Jesus Christ as "the Son of God," the eternal second person of the Trinity. He became a man, the "Christ" (Messiah), and offered Himself as a sacrifice for sins. Those who put their faith in Him will "have life in His name," while those who reject Him will be judged and sentenced to eternal punishment.

The reality that Jesus is God, introduced in the prologue, is expanded throughout the book by John's careful selection of claims and miracles that seal the case. Verses 1–3 of the prologue teach that Jesus is co-equal and co-eternal with the Father; verses 4 and 5 relate the salvation He brought, which was announced by His herald, John the Baptist (vv. 6–8); verses 9–13 describe the reaction of the human race to Him, either rejection (vv. 10–11) or acceptance (vv. 12–13); verses 14–18 summarize the entire prologue.

From the first five verses of John's gospel flow three evidences of the deity of the incarnate Word, Jesus Christ: His preexistence, His creative power, and His self-existence.

THE PREEXISTENCE OF THE WORD

In the beginning was the Word, and the Word was with God, and the Word was God. He was in the beginning with God. (1:1–2)

The Greek word translated "beginning" (*archē*) can mean "source," or "origin" (cf. Col. 1:18; Rev. 3:14); as well as "rule," "authority," "ruler," or "one in authority" (cf. Luke 12:11; 20:20; Rom. 8:38; 1 Cor. 15:24; Eph. 1:21; 3:10; 6:12; Col. 1:16; 2:10, 15; Titus 3:1). Both of those connotations are true of Christ, who is both the Creator of the universe (v. 3; Col. 1:16; Heb. 1:2), and its ruler (Col. 2:10; Eph. 1:20–22; Phil. 2:9–11). But the term refers here to the beginning of the universe depicted in Genesis 1:1.

Jesus Christ was already in existence when the heavens and the earth were created; thus, He is not a created being, but existed from all eternity. (Since time began with the creation of the physical universe, whatever existed before that creation is eternal.) "The Logos [Word] did not then begin to be, but at that point at which all else began to be, He already *was*. In the beginning, place it where you may, the Word already existed. In other words, the Logos is before time, eternal."[1] That truth provides powerful proof of Christ's deity, for only God is eternal.

The imperfect tense of the verb "was" (*eimi*), describing continuing action in the past, further reinforces the eternal preexistence of the Word. It indicates that the Word—Jesus—was continually in existence before the beginning. But even more significant is the use of the Greek word *eimi* instead of *ginomai* ("became"). The latter term refers to things that come into existence (cf. 1:3, 10, 12, 14). Had John used *ginomai,* he would have implied that the Word came into existence at the beginning along with the rest of creation. But *eimi* stresses that the Word always existed; there was never a point when He came into being.

The concept of "the Word" (*logos*) is one imbued with meaning for both Jews and Greeks. To the Greek philosophers, the *logos* was the impersonal, abstract principle of reason or order in the universe. It was in some sense a creative force, and also the source of wisdom. The average Greek may not have fully understood all the nuances of meaning with which the philosophers invested the term *logos.* Yet even to laypeople the term would have signified one of the most important principles in the universe.

To the Greeks, then, John presented Jesus as the personifica-tion and embodiment of the *logos*. Unlike the Greek concept, how-ever, Jesus was not an impersonal force, principle, or emanation. In Him, the true *logos*, who was God, became a man—a concept foreign to Greek thought.

But *logos* was not just a Greek concept. The word of the Lord was also a significant Old Testament theme, well-known to the Jews. The word of the Lord was the expression of divine power and wisdom. By speaking His word, God introduced the Abra-hamic covenant (Gen. 15:1), gave Israel the Ten Commandments (Ex. 24:3–4; Deut. 5:5; cf. Ex. 34:28; Deut. 9:10), attended the building of Solomon's temple (1 Kings 6:11–13), revealed God to Samuel (1 Sam. 3:21), pronounced judgment on the house of Eli (1 Kings 2:27), counseled Elijah (1 Kings 19:9ff.), directed Israel through God's spokesmen (cf. 1 Sam. 15:10; 2 Sam. 7:4ff.; 24:11ff.; 1 Kings 16:1–4; 17:2ff., 8ff.; 18:1; 21:17–18; 2 Chron. 11:2–4), was the agent of creation (Ps. 33:6), and revealed Scripture to many of the prophets, from Jeremiah to Malachi.[2]

The apostle John presented Jesus to his Jewish readers as the in-carnation of divine power and revelation. From John we learn that Jesus reveals God to man (John 1:18; 14:7–9), judges those who reject Him (John 3:18; 5:22), is the agent of creation (John 1:3; cf. Col. 1:16; Heb. 1:2), and will inspire the Scripture penned by the New Testament writers (John 14:26) through the Holy Spirit whom He promises to send (John 15:26).

Then John took his argument a step further. In His eternal preexistence "the Word was with God." The English translation does not bring out the full richness of the Greek expression (*pros ton theon*). That phrase means far more than merely that the Word existed with God; it "[gives] the picture of two personal beings facing one another and engaging in intelligent discourse."[3] From all eternity Jesus was "with the Father [*pros ton patera*]" (1 John 1:2) in deep, intimate fellowship. Perhaps *pros ton theon* could best be rendered "face to face." The Word is a person, not an attribute of God, or an emanation from Him. And He is of the same essence as the Father.

Yet in an act of infinite condescension, Jesus left the glory of heaven and the privilege of face-to-face communion with His Father (cf. John 17:5). He willingly "emptied Himself, taking the form of a bond-servant, and being made in the likeness of men. . . . He humbled Himself by becoming obedient to the point of death, even death on a cross" (Phil. 2:7–8). Charles Wesley captured some of the wonder of that marvelous truth in the familiar hymn, "And Can It Be That I Should Gain?":

> He left His Father's throne above,
> So free, so infinite His grace;
> Emptied Himself of all but love,
> And bled for Adam's helpless race.
>
> Amazing love! How can it be
> That Thou, my God, shouldst die for me?
> Amazing love! How can it be
> That Thou, my God, shouldst die for me?[4]

John's description of the Word reached its pinnacle in the final clause of this opening verse. Not only did the Word exist from all eternity, and have face-to-face fellowship with the Father, but also "the Word was God." That simple statement, only four words in both English and Greek (*theos ~en ho logos*), is perhaps the clearest and most direct declaration of the deity of the Lord Jesus Christ to be found anywhere in Scripture.

But despite their clarity, heretical groups almost from the moment John penned these words have twisted their meaning to support their false doctrines concerning the nature of the Lord Jesus Christ. Noting that the Greek term *theos* ("God") is anarthrous (not preceded by the definite article), some argue that it is an indefinite noun and mistranslate the phrase, "the Word was divine" (i.e., merely possessing some of the qualities of God) or, even more appalling, "the Word was *a* god."

The absence of the article before *theos,* however, does not make it indefinite. *Logos* ("Word") has the definite article to show that it is the subject of the sentence (since it is in the same case as *theos*). Thus the rendering "God was the Word," is invalid, because "the Word," not "God," is the subject. It would also be theologically incorrect, because it would equate the Father ("God" whom the Word was with in the preceding clause) with the Word, thus denying that the two are separate persons. The predicate nominative ("God") describes the nature of the Word, showing that He is of the same essence as the Father.[5]

According to the rules of Greek grammar, when the predicate nominative ("God" in this clause) precedes the verb, it cannot be considered indefinite (and thus translated "a god" instead of "God") merely because it does not have the article. That the term "God" is definite and refers to the true God is obvious for several reasons. First, *theos* appears without the definite article four other times in the immediate context (vv. 6, 12, 13, 18; cf. 3:2, 21; 9:16; Matt. 5:9). Not even the Jehovah's Witnesses' distorted translation of the Bible renders the anarthrous *theos* "a god" in those verses. Second, if John's meaning was that the Word was divine, or a god, there were ways he could have phrased it to make that unmistakably clear. For example, if he meant to say that the Word was merely in some sense divine, he could have used the adjective *theios* (cf. 2 Peter 1:4). It must be remembered that, as Robert L. Reymond notes, "No standard Greek lexicon offers 'divine' as one of the meanings of *theos,* nor does the noun become an adjective when it 'sheds' its article."[6] Or if John had wanted to say that the Word was a god, he could have written *ho logos ēn theos.* If the apostle had written *ho theos ēn ho logos,* the two nouns (*theos* and *logos*) would be interchangeable, and God and the Word would be identical. That would have meant that the Father was the Word, which, as noted above, would deny the Trinity. But as Leon Morris asks rhetorically, "How else [other than *theos ēn ho logos*] in Greek would one say, 'the Word was God'?"[7]

Under the inspiration of the Holy Spirit, John chose the precise wording that accurately conveys the true nature of the Word, Jesus Christ. "By *theos* without the article, John neither indicates, on the one hand, identity of Person with the Father; nor yet, on the other, any lower nature than that of God Himself."[8]

Underscoring their significance, John restated the profound truths of verse 1 in verse 2. He emphasized again the eternity of the Word; He already was in existence in the beginning when everything else was created. As it did in verse 1, the imperfect tense of the verb "was" (*eimi*) describes the Word's continuous existence before the beginning. And as John also noted in verse 1, that existence was one of intimate fellowship with God the Father.

The truth of Jesus Christ's deity and full equality with the Father is a nonnegotiable element of the Christian faith. In 2 John 10, John warned, "If anyone comes to you and does not bring this teaching [the biblical teaching concerning Christ; cf. vv. 7, 9], do not receive him into your house, and do not give him a greeting." Believers are not to aid heretical false teachers in any way, including giving them food and lodging, since the one who does so "participates in [their] evil deeds" (v. 11). Such seemingly uncharitable behavior is perfectly justified toward false teachers who deny the deity of our Lord and the gospel, since they are under God's curse:

> There are some who are disturbing you and want to distort the gospel of Christ. But even if we, or an angel from heaven, should preach to you a gospel contrary to what we have preached to you, he is to be accursed! As we have said before, so I say again now, if any man is preaching to you a gospel contrary to what you received, he is to be accursed! (Gal. 1:7–9)

Emphasizing their deadly danger, both Paul (Acts 20:29) and Jesus (Matt. 7:15) described false teachers as wolves in disguise. They are not to be welcomed into the sheepfold, but guarded against and avoided.

Confusion about the deity of Christ is inexcusable, because the biblical teaching regarding it is clear and unmistakable. Jesus Christ is the eternally preexistent Word, who enjoys face-to-face communion and divine life with the Father, and is Himself God.

The Creative Power of the Word

All things came into being through Him, and apart from Him nothing came into being that has come into being. (1:3)

Once again John expressed a profound truth in clear language. Jesus Christ, the eternal Word, created everything that came into being. John underscored that truth by repeating it negatively;

"apart from Him nothing [lit., "not even one thing"] came into being that has come into being."

That Jesus Christ created everything (cf. Col. 1:16; Heb. 1:2) offers two further proofs of His deity. First, the creator of all things must Himself be "uncreated"—one who never was created—and only God is uncreated. The Greek text emphasizes the distinction between the uncreated Word and His creation, since a different verb is used here than the one used in verses 1 and 2. As noted in the previous point, John used a form of the verb *eimi* ("to be"), which denotes a state of being, to describe the Word in verses 1 and 2; here, speaking of the creation of the universe, he used a form of the verb *ginomai* ("came into being"). That Jesus is the Creator also verifies His deity, because God is portrayed throughout the Bible as the Creator (Gen. 1:1; Ps. 102:25; Isa. 40:28; 42:5; 45:18; Mark 13:19; Rom. 1:25; Eph. 3:9; Rev. 4:11).

By stressing the role of the Word in creating the universe, John countered the false teaching that later developed into the dangerous heresy known as Gnosticism. The Gnostics embraced the philosophical dualism common to Greek philosophy that held that spirit was good and matter was evil. They argued that since matter was evil, the good God could not have created the physical universe. Instead, a series of spirit beings emanated from Him until finally one of those descending emanations was evil and foolish enough to create the physical universe. But John rejected that heretical view, strongly affirming that Jesus Christ was the Father's agent in creating everything.

The present world, however, is radically different from God's original good creation (Gen. 1:31). The catastrophic results of the fall not only affected the human race, but also the entire creation.

Jesus therefore will one day redeem not only believers, but also the material world as well, as Paul noted in Romans 8:19–21:

> For the anxious longing of the creation waits eagerly for the revealing of the sons of God. For the creation was subjected to futility, not willingly, but because of Him who subjected it, in hope that the creation itself also will be set free from its slavery to corruption into the freedom of the glory of the children of God.

When the curse is lifted during Christ's millennial reign,

> The wolf will dwell with the lamb,
> And the leopard will lie down with the young goat,
> And the calf and the young lion and the fatling together;
> And a little boy will lead them.
> Also the cow and the bear will graze,
> Their young will lie down together,
> And the lion will eat straw like the ox.
> The nursing child will play by the hole of the cobra,
> And the weaned child will put his hand on the viper's den.
> They will not hurt or destroy in all My holy mountain,
> For the earth will be full of the knowledge of the LORD
> As the waters cover the sea. (Isa. 11:6–9)

"The wolf and the lamb will graze together, and the lion will eat straw like the ox; and dust will be the serpent's food. They will do no evil or harm in all My holy mountain," says the LORD. (Isa. 65:25)

THE SELF-EXISTENCE OF THE WORD

In Him was life, and the life was the Light of men. The Light shines in the darkness, and the darkness did not comprehend it. (1:4–5)

Displaying yet again his Spirit-inspired economy of words, John in these two brief verses summarized the incarnation. Christ, the embodiment of life and the glorious, eternal Light of heaven, entered the sin-darkened world of men, and that world reacted in various ways to Him.

The themes of life and light are common in John's gospel. "Life" (from the Greek *zōē*) refers to spiritual life as opposed to the Greek term *bios,* which describes physical life (e.g., 1 John 2:16). Here, as in 5:26, it refers primarily to Christ having life in Himself. Theologians refer to that as "aseity," or self-existence. It is clear evidence of Christ's deity, since only God is self-existent.

This truth of God's and Christ's self-existence—having life in themselves—is foundational to our faith. All that is created can be said to be "becoming," because nothing created is unchanging. It is essential to understand that permanent, eternal, non-changing being or life is distinct from all that is becoming. "Being" is eternal and the source of life for what is "becoming." That is what distinguishes creatures from the Creator, us from God.

Genesis 1:1 establishes this fundamental reality with the statement, "In the beginning God created the heavens and the earth." Because it is the most important truth in the Bible, it is the one most assaulted. Unbelievers know that to be rid of creation is to be rid of a Creator. And to be rid of God leaves men free to live in whatever way they want, with no judgment.

The whole universe falls into the category of "becoming" because there was a point when it did not exist. But there was never a point when God did not exist. All creation receives its life from outside, from God, but He derives His life from within Himself, depending on nothing for His self-existence. As He declared to Moses, "I am who I am" (Ex. 3:14). He is from everlasting to everlasting. Acts 17:28 rightly says: "In Him we live and move and exist." We cannot live or move or be without His life. But He has always lived and moved and been.

This is the purest ontological description of God—and to say Jesus is the life is to say the purest truth about the nature of God that He possesses. And, as in verse 3, He then is the Creator.

While as the creator Jesus is the source of everything and everyone who lives, the word "life" in John's gospel always translates *zōē,* which John uses for spiritual or eternal life. It is imparted by God's sovereign grace (6:37, 39, 44, 65; cf. Eph. 2:8) to all those who believe in Jesus Christ as Savior (1:12; 3:15, 16, 36; 6:40, 47; 20:31; cf. Acts 16:31; Rom. 10:9–10; 1 John 5:1, 11–13). It was to impart spiritual life to sinners who "were dead in [their] trespasses and sins" (Eph. 2:1) that Jesus came into the world (10:10; cf. 6:33).

While it is appropriate to make some distinction between life and light, the statement "the life was the Light" halts any disconnect between the two. In reality, John is writing that the life and light cannot be separated. They are essentially the same, with the idea of light emphasizing the manifestation of the divine life. "The life was the Light" is the same construction as "the Word was God" (v. 1). As God is not separate from the Word, but the same in essence, so life and light share the same essential properties.

The light combines with life in a metaphor for the purpose of clarity and contrast. God's life is true and holy. Light is that truth and holiness manifest against the darkness of lies and sin. Light and life are linked in this same way in John 8:12, in which Jesus says: "I am the Light of the world; he who follows Me will not walk in the darkness, but will have the Light of life." The connection between light and life is also clearly made in the Old Testament. Psalm 36:9 says, "For with You is the fountain of life; in Your light we see light."

"The light of the gospel of the glory of Christ, who is the image of God" (2 Cor. 4:4) is nothing more than the radiating, manifest life of God shining in His Son. Paul specifically says: "God . . . is the One who has shone in our hearts to give the Light of the knowledge of the glory of God in the face of Christ" (v. 6). So light is God's life manifest in Christ.

In addition to its connection to life, light carries its own significance, as seen in the contrast between light and darkness, which is a common theme in Scripture. Intellectually, light refers to truth (Ps. 119:105; Prov. 6:23; 2 Cor. 4:4) and darkness to falsehood (Rom. 2:19); morally, light refers to holiness (Rom. 13:12; 2 Cor. 6:14; Eph. 5:8; 1 Thess. 5:5) and darkness to sin (Prov. 4:19; Isa. 5:20; Acts 26:18;). Satan's kingdom is the "domain of darkness" (Col. 1:13; cf. Luke 22:53; Eph. 6:12), but Jesus is the source of life (11:25; 14:6; cf. Acts 3:15; 1 John 1:1) and the light that shines in the darkness of the lost world (8:12; 9:5; 12:35–36, 46).

Despite Satan's frantic, furious assaults on the Light, "the darkness did not comprehend it." The word "comprehend" (*katalambanō*) is better translated "overcome." Even a small candle can drive the darkness from a room; the brilliant, glorious light of the Lord Jesus Christ will utterly destroy Satan's realm of darkness. Since He came into the world, "the darkness is passing away and the true Light is already shining" (1 John 2:8).

The thrust of this verse, then, is not that the darkness failed to understand the truth about Jesus; on the contrary, the forces of darkness know Him all too well. In Matthew 8:29 some demons "cried out [to Jesus], saying, 'What business do we have with each other, Son of God? Have You come here to torment us before the time?'" In Peter's house in Capernaum, Jesus "cast out many demons; and He was not permitting the demons to speak, because they knew who He was" (Mark 1:34). Luke 4:41 records that "demons also were coming out of many, shouting, 'You are the Son of God!' But rebuking them, He would not allow them to speak, because they knew Him to be the Christ." In Luke 4:34 a terrified demon pleaded, "Let us alone! What business do we have with each other, Jesus of Nazareth? Have You come to destroy us? I know who You are—the Holy One of God!" The demons not only know the truth about Christ, they also believe it. "You believe that God is one," wrote James, "You do well; the demons also believe, and shudder" (James 2:19).

It is because they understand with total clarity the judgment that awaits them that Satan and the demons have tried desperately throughout history to extinguish the light. In the Old Testament, Satan tried to destroy Israel, the nation from which the Messiah would come. He also tried to destroy the kingly line from which the Messiah would descend (2 Kings 11:1-2). In the New Testament, he prompted Herod's futile attempt to kill the infant Jesus (Matt. 2:16). At the beginning of His earthly ministry, Satan vainly tried to tempt Jesus to turn aside from the cross (Matt. 4:1-11). Later, he repeated the temptation again through one of His closest followers (Matt. 16:21-23). Even Satan's seeming triumph at the cross in reality marked his ultimate defeat (Col. 2:15; Heb. 2:14; cf. 1 John 3:8).

Similarly, unbelievers are eternally lost not because they do not know the truth, but because they reject it:

For the wrath of God is revealed from heaven against all ungodliness and unrighteousness of men who suppress the truth in unrighteousness, because that which is known about God is evident within them; for God made it evident to them. For since the creation of the world His invisible attributes, His eternal power and divine nature, have been clearly seen, being understood through what has been made, so that they are without excuse. For even though they knew God, they did not honor Him as God or give thanks, but they became futile in their speculations, and their foolish heart was darkened. (Rom. 1:18–21)

No one who rejects Christ's deity can be saved, for He Himself said in John 8:24, "Therefore I said to you that you will die in your sins; for unless you believe that I am He, you will die in your sins." It is fitting, then, that John opens his gospel, which so strongly emphasizes Christ's deity (cf. 8:58; 10:28–30; 20:28), with a powerful affirmation of that essential truth.

⎯⎯⎯⎯~⟨∞⟩~⎯⎯⎯⎯

Chapter 2

THE GLORIOUS PREEMINENCE OF JESUS CHRIST

Colossians 1:15–19

He is the image of the invisible God, the firstborn of all creation. For by Him all things were created, both in the heavens and on earth, visible and invisible, whether thrones or dominions or rulers or authorities—all things have been created through Him and for Him. He is before all things, and in Him all things hold together. He is also head of the body, the church; and He is the beginning, the firstborn from the dead, so that He Himself will come to have first place in everything. For it was the Father's good pleasure for all the fullness to dwell in Him. (1:15–19)

The Bible is supremely the book about the Lord Jesus Christ. The Old Testament records the preparation for His coming. The Gospels present Him as God in human flesh, come into the world to save sinners. In Acts, the message of salvation in Christ begins to be spread throughout the world. The epistles detail the theology of Christ's work and personification of Christ in His Body, the church. Finally, Revelation presents Christ on the throne, reigning as King of Kings and Lord of Lords.

Every part of Scripture testifies about Jesus Christ. Luke 24:27 says, "Then beginning with Moses and with all the prophets, [Jesus] explained to them the things concerning Himself in all the Scriptures." In John 5:39, Jesus said of the Scriptures, "It is these that testify about Me." Philip preached Christ to the Ethiopian eunuch by using the book of Isaiah (Acts 8:35).

But of all the Bible's teaching about Jesus Christ, none is more significant than Colossians 1:15–19. This dramatic and powerful passage removes any doubt or confusion over Jesus' true identity. It is vital to a proper understanding of the Christian faith.

Much of the heresy threatening the Colossian church centered on the Person of Christ. The heretics, denying His humanity, viewed Christ as one of many lesser descending spirit beings that emanated from God. They taught a form of philosophic dualism, postulating that spirit was good and matter was evil. Hence, a good emanation like Christ could never take on a body composed of evil matter. The idea that God Himself could become man was absurd to them. Thus, they also denied His deity.

Nor was Christ adequate for salvation, according to the errorists. Salvation required a superior, mystical, secret knowledge, beyond that of the gospel of Christ. It also involved worshiping the good emanations (angels) and keeping the Jewish ceremonial laws.

In Colossians 1–3, Paul confronts the Colossian heresy head-on. He rejects their denial of Christ's humanity, pointing out that it is in Him that "all the fullness of Deity dwells in bodily form" (2:9). Paul also rejects their worship of angels (2:18) and their ceremonialism (2:16–17). He emphatically denies that any secret knowledge is required for salvation, pointing out that in Christ "are hidden all the treasures of wisdom and knowledge" (2:3; cf. 1:27; 3:1–4).

By far the most serious aspect of the Colossian heresy was its rejection of Christ's deity. Before getting to the other issues, the apostle Paul makes an emphatic defense of that crucial doctrine. Christians would do well to follow his example in their confrontations with cultists. The primary focus of discussions with them should be the deity of Jesus Christ.

In Colossians 1:15–19, Paul reveals our Lord's true identity by viewing Him in relation to four things: God, the universe, the unseen world, and the church.

JESUS CHRIST IN RELATION TO GOD

He is the image of the invisible God, the firstborn of all creation. (1:15)

As already noted, the heretics viewed Jesus as one among a series of lesser spirits descending in sequential inferiority from God. Paul refutes that with two powerful descriptions of who Jesus really is. First, Paul describes Him as "the image of the invisible God." The word translated "image" (*eikōn*) can also be rendered as "likeness." From it we get our English word "icon," referring to a statue. It is used in Matthew 22:20 of Caesar's portrait on a coin, and in Revelation 13:14 of the statue of Antichrist.

Although man is created in the image of God (1 Cor. 11:7; cf. Gen. 1:26–27), man is not a perfect image of God. Humans are made in God's image in that they have rational personality. Like God, they possess intellect, emotion, and will, by which they are able to think, feel, and choose. We humans are not, however, in God's image morally, because He is holy, and we are sinful. Nor are we created in His image essentially. We do not possess His incommunicable attributes, such as omniscience, omnipotence, immutability, or omnipresence. We are human, not divine.

The fall marred the original image of God in man. Before the fall, Adam and Eve were innocent, free of sin, and incapable of dying. They forfeited those qualities when they sinned. When someone puts faith in Christ, however, that person is promised that the image of God will be restored in him or her. "For those whom He foreknew, He also predestined to become conformed to the image of His Son" (Rom. 8:29; cf. 2 Cor. 3:18; Col. 3:10). God will make believers sinless like Christ when they enter the final phase of their eternal life.

Unlike man, Jesus Christ is the perfect, absolutely accurate image of God. He did not become the image of God at the incarnation, but has been that from all eternity. Hebrews 1:3 describes Jesus as "the radiance of [God's] glory." Christ reflects God's attributes, as the sun's light reflects the sun. Further, He is said to be "the exact representation of [God's] nature." The Greek word *charaktēr* ("exact representation") refers to an engraving tool, or stamp. Jesus is the exact likeness of God. He is in the very form of God (Phil. 2:6). That is why He could say, "He who has seen Me has seen the Father" (John 14:9). In Christ, the invisible God became visible, "and we saw His glory, glory as of the only begotten from the Father" (John 1:14).

By using the term *eikōn*, Paul emphasizes that Jesus is both the representation and manifestation of God. He is the final and complete revelation of God. Indeed, He *is* God in human flesh. That was His claim (John 8:58; 10:30–33), and the unanimous testimony of Scripture (cf. John 1:1; 20:28; Rom. 9:5; Phil. 2:6; Col. 2:9; Titus 2:13; Heb. 1:8; 2 Peter 1:1). To think anything less of Him is blasphemy and gives evidence of a mind blinded by Satan (2 Cor. 4:4).

Paul further describes Jesus as the "firstborn of all creation." From the Arians of the early church to the Jehovah's Witnesses of our own day, those who would deny our Lord's deity have sought support from this phrase. They argue that it speaks of Christ as a created being, and hence He could not be the eternal God. Such an interpretation completely misunderstands the sense of "firstborn" (*prōtotokos*) and ignores the context.

Although the Greek word *prōtotokos* can mean firstborn chronologically (Luke 2:7), it refers primarily to position, or rank. In both Greek and Jewish culture, the firstborn was the son who had the right of inheritance. He was not necessarily the first one born. Although Esau was born first chronologically, it was Jacob who was the "firstborn" and received the inheritance. Jesus is the One with the right to the inheritance of all creation (cf. Heb. 1:2; Rev. 5:1–7, 13).

Israel was called God's firstborn in Exodus 4:22 and Jeremiah 31:9. Though not the first people born, they held first place in God's sight among all the nations. In Psalm 89:27, God says of the Messiah, "I also shall make him My firstborn," then defines what He means—"the highest of the kings of the earth." In Revelation 1:5, Jesus is called "the firstborn of the dead," even though He was not the first person to be resurrected chronologically. Of all ever raised, He is the preeminent One. Romans 8:29 refers to Him as the firstborn in relation to the church. In all the above cases, firstborn clearly means highest in rank, not the first created.

There are many other reasons for rejecting the idea that the use of "firstborn" makes Jesus a created being. Such an interpretation cannot be harmonized with the description of Jesus as "only begotten," or "unique" (*monogenēs*), in John 1:18. We might well ask with the early church father Theodoret how, if Christ was only begotten, could He be first-begotten? And how, if He were first-begotten, could He be only begotten? How could He be the first of many in His class, and at the same time the only member of His class? Yet such confusion is inevitable if we assign the meaning "first created" to "firstborn." Further, when the Greek term *prōtotokos* is one of the class referred to, the class is plural (cf. Col. 1:18; Rom. 8:29). Yet, creation is singular. Finally, if Paul meant to convey that Christ was the first created being, why did he not use the Greek word *prōtoktistos*, which means "first created"?

Such an interpretation of "firstborn" is also foreign to the context—both the general context of the epistle and the specific context of the passage. If Paul were here teaching that Christ is a created being, he would be agreeing with the central point of the Colossian errorists. They taught that Christ was a created being, the most prominent of the emanations from God. That would run counter to his purpose in writing Colossians, which was to refute the false teachers at Colossae.

Interpreting "firstborn" to mean that Christ is a created being is also out of harmony with the immediate context. Paul has just finished describing Christ as the perfect and complete image of God. In the next verse, he refers to Christ as the creator of everything that exists. How then could Christ Himself be a created being? Further, verse 17 states, "He is before all things." Christ existed before anything else was created (cf. Micah 5:2), and only God existed before the creation.

Far from being one of a series of emanations descending from God, Jesus is the perfect image of God. He is the preeminent inheritor over all creation. (The genitive *ktiseōs* is better translated "over" than "of.") He both existed before the creation and is exalted in rank above it. Those truths define who Jesus is in relation to God. They also devastate the false teachers' position. But Paul is not finished—his next point undermines another false teaching of the Colossian errorists.

JESUS CHRIST IN
RELATION TO THE UNIVERSE

For by Him all things were created, both in the heavens and on earth, visible and invisible, whether thrones or dominions or rulers or authorities—all things have been created through Him and for Him. He is before all things, and in Him all things hold together. (1:16–17)

Paul gives three reasons for Jesus' primacy over creation. First, He is the Creator. The false teachers at Colossae viewed Jesus as the first and most important of the emanations from God, but they were convinced it had to be a lesser being much further down the chain who eventually created the material universe. But Paul rejects that blasphemy, insisting that by Him all things were created. That truth is affirmed by the apostle John (John 1:3) and the writer of Hebrews (Heb. 1:2). Because the Colossian errorists viewed matter as evil, they argued that neither the good God nor a good emanation could have created it. But Paul maintains that Jesus made all things, both in the heavens and on earth, visible and invisible. He refutes the false philosophic dualism of the Colossian heresy. Jesus is God, and He created the material universe.

The Power and Wisdom of the Creator

By studying the creation, one can gain a glimpse of the power, knowledge, and wisdom of the Creator. The sheer size of the universe is staggering. The sun, for example, has a diameter of 864,000 miles (one hundred times that of earth's) and could hold 1.3 million planets the size of earth inside it. The star Betelgeuse, however, has a diameter of 100 million miles, which is larger than the earth's orbit around the sun. It takes sunlight, traveling at 186,000 miles per second, about 8.5 minutes to reach earth. Yet that same light would take more than four years to reach the nearest star system, Alpha Centauri, some 25 trillion miles from earth. The galaxy to which our sun belongs, the Milky Way, contains hundreds of billions of stars. And astronomers estimate there are millions, or even billions of galaxies. What they can see leads them to estimate the number of stars in the universe at 10^{25}, that is, ten to the twenty-fifth power! That is roughly the number of all the grains of sand on all the world's beaches.

The universe also bears witness to the tremendous wisdom and knowledge of its Creator. Scientists now speak of the Anthropic Principle, "which states that the universe appears to be carefully designed for the well-being of mankind."[1] A change in the rate of the Earth's rotation around the sun or on its axis would be catastrophic. The Earth would become either too hot or too cold to support life. If the moon were much nearer to the Earth, huge tides would inundate the continents. A change in the composition of the gases that make up our atmosphere would also be fatal to life. A slight change in the mass of the proton would result in the dissolution of hydrogen atoms. That would result in the destruction of the universe, because hydrogen is its dominant element.

The creation gives silent testimony to the intelligence of its Creator. Max Planck, winner of the 1918 Nobel Prize in physics and regarded as one of the founders of modern physics, wrote:

> According to everything taught by the exact sciences about the immense realm of nature, a certain order prevails—one independent of the human mind . . . [and] this order can be formulated in terms of purposeful activity. There is evidence of an intelligent order of the universe to which both man and nature are subservient."[2]

A Declaration of God by His Creation

It is no wonder that the psalmist wrote, "The heavens are telling of the glory of God; and their expanse is declaring the work of His hands. Day to day pours forth speech, and night to night reveals knowledge. There is no speech, nor are there words; their voice is not heard. Their line has gone out through all the earth, and their utterances to the end of the world" (Ps. 19:1–4).

The testimony of nature to its Creator is so clear that it is only through willful unbelief that men can reject it. Paul writes in Romans 1:20, "For since the creation of the world His invisible attributes, His eternal power and divine nature, have been clearly seen, being understood through what has been made, so that they are without excuse." Like those who deny Christ's deity, those who reject Him as Creator give evidence of a mind darkened by sin and blinded by Satan.

The Sustaining of Creation by Jesus

Jesus also has primacy over the creation because He is before all things. When the universe began, He already existed (John 1:1–2; 1 John 1:1). He told the Jews in John 8:58, "Before Abraham was born, I am" (not "I was"). He is saying that He is Yahweh, the eternally existing God. The prophet Micah said of Him, "His goings forth are from long ago, from the days of eternity" (Mic. 5:2). Revelation 22:13 describes Him as "the Alpha and the Omega, the first and the last, the beginning and the end." As was previously mentioned, anyone existing before time began at the creation is eternal, and only God is eternal.

A third reason for Jesus' primacy over creation is that in Him all things hold together. Not only did Jesus create the universe, He also sustains it. He maintains the delicate balance necessary to life's existence. He quite literally holds all things together. He is the power behind every consistency in the universe. He is gravity and centrifugal and centripetal force. He is the One who keeps all the entities in space in their motion. He is the energy of the universe. In his book *The Atom Speaks*, D. Lee Chesnut describes the puzzle of why the nucleus of the atom holds together:

> Consider the dilemma of the nuclear physicist when he finally looks in utter amazement at the pattern he had now drawn of the oxygen nucleus.... For here are eight positively charged protons closely associated together within the confines of this tiny nucleus. With them are eight neutrons—a total of sixteen particles—eight positively charged, eight with no charge.
>
> Earlier physicists had discovered that like charges of electricity and like magnetic poles repel each other, and unlike charges or magnetic poles attract each other. And the entire history of electrical phenomena and electrical equipment had been built up on these principles known as Coulomb's law of electrostatic force and the law of magnetism. What was wrong? What holds the nucleus together? Why doesn't it fly apart? And therefore, why do not all atoms fly apart?[3]

Chesnut goes on to describe the experiments performed in the 1920s and 1930s that proved Coulomb's law applied to atomic nuclei. Powerful "atom smashers" were used to fire protons into the nuclei of atoms. Those experiments also gave scientists an understanding of the incredibly powerful force that held protons together within the nucleus. Scientists have dubbed that force the "strong nuclear force," but have no explanation for why it exists. The physicist George Gamow, one of the founders of the Big Bang theory of the origin of the universe, wrote, "The fact that we live in a world in which practically every object is a potential nuclear explosive, without being blown to bits, is due to the extreme difficulties that attend the starting of a nuclear reaction."[4] Physicist Karl K. Darrow agrees:

> You grasp what this implies. It implies that all the massive nuclei have no right to be alive at all. Indeed, they should never have been created, and, if created, they should have blown up instantly. Yet here they all are. . . . Some inflexible inhibition is holding them relentlessly together. The nature of the inhibition is also a secret . . . one thus far reserved by Nature for herself.[5]

One day in the future God will dissolve the strong nuclear force. The apostle Peter describes that day as the one when "the heavens will pass away with a roar and the elements will be destroyed with intense heat, and the earth and its works will be burned up" (2 Peter 3:10). With the strong nuclear force no longer operative, Coulomb's law will take effect, and the nuclei of atoms will fly apart. The universe will literally explode. Until that time, we can be thankful that Christ "upholds all things by the word of His power" (Heb. 1:3). Jesus Christ must be God. He made the universe, existed outside and before it, and preserves it.

Jesus Christ in Relation to the Unseen World

whether thrones or dominions or rulers or authorities (1:16b)

"Thrones or dominions or rulers or authorities" refer to the various ranks of angels. Far from being an angel, as the Colossian errorists taught, Jesus Christ created the angels. The writer of

Hebrews also makes a clear distinction between Christ and the angels: "Of the angels He says, 'Who makes His angels winds, and His ministers a flame of fire.' But of the Son He says, 'Your throne, O God, is forever and ever, and the righteous scepter is the scepter of His kingdom'" (Heb. 1:7–8). Jesus has been exalted "far above all rule and authority and power and dominion, and every name that is named, not only in this age but also in the one to come" (Eph. 1:21). As a result, "At the name of Jesus every knee will bow, of those who are in heaven and on earth and under the earth" (Phil. 2:10). With that truth the apostle Peter agrees: "[Christ] is at the right hand of God, having gone into heaven, after angels and authorities and powers had been subjected to Him" (1 Peter 3:22).

Scripture is clear that Jesus is not an angel, but the Creator of the angels. He is above the angels, who in fact worship Him and are under His authority. Jesus' relation to the unseen world, like His relation to the visible universe, proves He is God.

JESUS CHRIST IN RELATION TO THE CHURCH

He is also head of the body, the church; and He is the beginning, the firstborn from the dead, so that He Himself will come to have first place in everything. For it was the Father's good pleasure for all the fullness to dwell in Him (1:18–19)

Paul presents four great truths in this verse about Christ's relation to the church.

Christ Is the Head of the Church

There are many metaphors used in Scripture to describe the church. It is called a family, a kingdom, a vineyard, a flock, a building, and a bride. But the most profound metaphor, one having no

Old Testament equivalent, is that of a body. The church is a body, known as the Body of Christ, and He is its head. This concept is not used in the sense of the head of a company, but rather looks at the church as a living organism, inseparably tied together by the living Christ. He controls every part of it and gives it life and direction. His life lived out through all the members provides the unity of the Body (cf. 1 Cor. 12:12–20). He energizes and coordinates the diversity within the Body, a diversity of spiritual gifts and ministries (1 Cor. 12:4–13). He also directs the Body's mutuality, as the individual members serve and support each other (1 Cor. 12:15–27).

Christ is not an angel who serves the church (cf. Heb. 1:14). He is the head of His church.

Christ Is the Source of the Church

The word "beginning" (*archē*) is used here in the twofold sense of source and primacy. The church has its origins in Jesus. God "chose us in Him before the foundation of the world" (Eph. 1:4). It is He who gives life to His church. His sacrificial death and resurrection on our behalf provided our new life. As head of the Body, Jesus holds the chief position, or highest rank in the church. As the beginning, He is its originator.

Christ Is the Firstborn from the Dead

"Firstborn" again translates the Greek word *prōtotokos*. Of all those who have been raised from the dead, or ever will be, Christ is the highest in rank.

Christ Is the Preeminent One

As a result of His death and resurrection, Jesus has come to have first place in everything. Paul summarizes for emphasis in verse 18. He wants to drive home the point as forcefully as he can that Jesus is not merely another emanation from God. Because

> He humbled Himself by becoming obedient to the point of death, even death on a cross. For this reason also, God highly exalted Him, and bestowed on Him the name which is above every name, so that at the name of Jesus every knee will bow, of those who are in heaven and on earth and under the earth, and that every tongue will confess that Jesus Christ is Lord, to the glory of God the Father. (Phil. 2:8–11)

Jesus reigns supreme over the visible world, the unseen world, and the church. Paul sums up his argument in verse 19: "For it was the Father's good pleasure for all the fullness to dwell in Him." The word translated "fullness" (*plērōma*) was a term used by the later Gnostics to refer to the divine powers and attributes, which they believed were divided among the various emanations. That is likely the sense in which the Colossian errorists used the term. Paul counters that false teaching by stating that all the fullness of deity is not spread out in small doses to a group of spirits, but fully dwells in Christ alone (cf. 2:9). The commentator J. B. Lightfoot wrote about Paul's use of *plērōma*,

> On the one hand, in relation to Deity, He is the visible image of the invisible God. He is not only the chief manifestation of the Divine nature: He exhausts the Godhead manifested. In Him resides the totality of the Divine powers and attributes. For this totality Gnostic teachers had a technical term, the *pleroma* or plenitude. . . . In contrast to their doctrine, [Paul] asserts and repeats the assertion, that the *pleroma* abides absolutely and wholly in Christ as the Word of God. The entire light is concentrated in Him.[6]

Paul tells the Colossians they do not need angels to help them enter heaven. Rather in Christ, and Him alone, they are complete before God (2:10). Christians share in His fullness: "For of His fullness we have all received, and grace upon grace" (John 1:16). All the fullness of Christ becomes available to believers.

What should the response be to the glorious truths about Christ in this passage? The Puritan John Owen astutely wrote,

> The revelation made of Christ in the blessed gospel is far more excellent, more glorious, more filled with rays of divine wisdom and goodness than the whole creation, and the just comprehension of it, if attainable, can contain or afford. Without this knowledge, the mind of man, however priding itself in other inventions and discoveries, is wrapped up in darkness and confusion.
>
> This therefore deserves the severest of our thoughts, the best of our meditations, and our utmost diligence in them. For if our future blessedness shall consist in living where He is, and beholding of His glory, what better preparation can there be for it than a constant previous contemplation of that glory as revealed in the gospel, that by a view of it we may be gradually transformed into the same glory?[7]

PART 2

THE DIVINE
AUTHORITY OF
CHRIST

Chapter 3

———— ⚬∞⚬ ————

CHRIST'S AUTHORITY OVER SATAN AND DEMONS

MARK 1:21–28

They went into Capernaum; and immediately on the Sabbath He entered the synagogue and began to teach. They were amazed at His teaching; for He was teaching them as one having authority, and not as the scribes. Just then there was a man in their synagogue with an unclean spirit; and he cried out, saying, "What business do we have with each other, Jesus of Nazareth? Have You come to destroy us? I know who You are—the Holy One of God!" And Jesus rebuked him, saying, "Be quiet, and come out of him!" Throwing him into convulsions, the unclean spirit cried out with a loud voice and came out of him. They were all amazed, so that they debated among themselves, saying, "What is this? A new teaching with authority! He commands even the unclean spirits, and they obey Him." Immediately the news about Him spread everywhere into all the surrounding district of Galilee. (1:21–28)

Life's most critical question is, "Who is Jesus Christ?" Knowing the truth about Jesus is essential, both for this life and the life to come. Yet few seem seriously interested in rightly understanding who He is and why He came. Tragically, many people blindly assume that Jesus was merely a good teacher, a moral idealist, or a misunderstood social activist whose life ended in tragedy two millennia ago. But that is not how Scripture presents Him, nor is it in keeping with whom He declared Himself to be.

The gospel of Mark (like the other three Gospels) provides a definitive answer to that question. In the very first verse, Mark declares Jesus to be the Christ—the messianic King—and the Son of God. He is the divinely-appointed ruler to whom all the prerogatives of royalty are due. Moreover, He is God incarnate, worthy of all glory, honor, and praise. He is the Lord of lords, possessing all authority both in heaven and on earth (cf. Matt. 28:18). Consequently, the only right response to His sovereign dominion is to submit and worship Him as the eternal King of Kings and the glorious Son of God.

Any depiction of Jesus that undermines or belittles His true person and position is not only inadequate, but also blasphemous. Though many demean and disparage Him now, all will one day recognize Him for who He truly is. As the apostle Paul told the Philippians, "At the name of Jesus every knee will bow, of those who are in heaven and on earth and under the earth, and . . . every tongue will confess that Jesus Christ is Lord, to the glory of God the Father" (Phil. 2:10–11).

Mark 1:21–28 is a passage that dramatically illustrates both the sovereign authority of Jesus Christ and the stubborn unwillingness of unbelieving sinners to recognize and submit to that authority. The passage comes on the heels of Mark's introduction (in vv.

1–20), in which he presented five proofs to demonstrate that Jesus is indeed the divine King: Jesus was preceded by a royal forerunner (1:2–8), experienced a divine coronation ceremony (1:9–11), defeated His archenemy the prince of darkness (1:12–13), proclaimed the kingdom message of salvation (1:14–15), and commanded His kingdom citizens to follow Him (1:16–20). Heralded by John, commissioned by the Father, filled with the Spirit, victorious over sin and Satan, and accompanied by His disciples—the Lord Jesus began His public ministry with every necessary credential demonstrated.

So, succinctly but convincingly, Mark's fast-moving, condensed, and selective introduction established the messianic character and divine nature of the Lord Jesus. Now, as Mark begins the body of his gospel record, he will slow his pace to focus more intently on specific events from the ministry of the messianic King.

A Dramatic Showdown with a Demon

The history begins in verse 21 with the inspired recounting of an incident in which Jesus demonstrated His authority over the demonic realm. Mark has already highlighted Christ's authority over Satan and sin. Now He gathers His first disciples (verses 12–20). In this section (vv. 21–28) Mark specifically focuses on a dramatic showdown one Sabbath day between Jesus and a demon. Once again, the cosmic authority of Jesus is vividly put on display, leaving no doubt about the King's ability to dominate demons and to obliterate the satanic bondage that can hold sinners captive all the way to hell.

A Striking Contrast in Responses

The passage itself reveals a striking contrast between the response of people to Jesus' authority and the response of demons. On the one hand, people were amazed at Jesus' power and authority (vv. 22, 27). They reacted with wonder, curiosity, and surprise because He taught as no one they had ever heard before. On the other hand, demons were terrified by Christ. They responded in horror, dread, and panic. Those divergent reactions lie at the heart of understanding the significance of this passage. Both the demons and the people were sinful. Yet only the demons shrieked in fear. They understood Jesus was their Judge who would cast them into hell. The people certainly did not.

Ironically, in the first half of Mark's gospel, the only beings sure of Jesus' true identity were the demons. The Jewish leaders rejected Him (3:6, 22); the crowds were curious but largely uncommitted (6:5–6; cf. John 2:24); and even His disciples exhibited a lingering hardheartedness (8:17). But the demons knew for certain. As Mark explains, "Whenever the unclean spirits saw Him, they would fall down before Him and shout, 'You are the Son of God!'" (3:11). Knowing exactly who Jesus was and what He had the power to do, they responded with terror—fearing He might cast them immediately into the abyss (Luke 8:31; cf. Rev. 9:1). As one unclean spirit cried out, "What business do we have with each other, Jesus, Son of the Most High God? I implore You by God, do not torment me!" (5:7). They had known the Son of God since He created them (Col. 1:16). Their ancient minds were full of the particulars about their heavenly rebellion, defeat, and expulsion; and they understood the eternal punishment that yet awaits them in the lake of fire (Matt. 25:41). Understandably, the demons were utterly terrified in Jesus' presence. Now that the Son had come to earth to begin the establishment of His rule, the evil angels had every reason to be tormented by terror.

There is no salvation for fallen angels (Heb. 2:16). However, sinners who come to a true understanding of the authority of the Son of God and are terrified by the threat of hell are invited to flee from wrath and run in holy fear to Christ for the forgiveness and grace of salvation. Yet the vast majority of sinners who hear the good news of heaven still refuse to fear hell and come to Christ for the gift of salvation. Such is the great irony depicted by this passage. The demons recognized who Jesus was, but have no possibility of salvation. The crowds were offered divine forgiveness, but they refused to recognize the One who alone can provide it. Put another way, the demons were terrified and could not be saved; the people were amazed and would not be saved. Consequently, the amazed people (who would not believe) and the terrified demons (who do "believe, and shudder"—James 2:19) will ultimately end up in the same eternal lake of fire (Rev. 20:10–15).

It is important to emphasize that during Jesus' ministry, the demons did not attack Him. They assaulted the souls of sinful people, but never Jesus. In fact, whenever a confrontation occurred, it was Jesus who attacked them. His mere presence sent them into a frenzied panic. Though invisible to the naked eye, they were not invisible to Him. They might be able to hide from people—disguising themselves as angels of light (2 Cor. 11:4) and dwelling comfortably within the confines of apostate religion. But they could not hide from the omniscient gaze of Christ. In His presence, they blew their cover due to the constraining power of their fear.

Jesus' Absolute Power over the Demons and Satan

Throughout His entire ministry, Jesus' dominance over the demons was absolute and uncontested—indicative of the fact that He possessed absolute power over the devil and the entire force of fallen angels in the domain of darkness (Col. 1:13). He is able to overwhelm Satan—the one who controls this world system (1 John 5:19) and who has blinded sinners (2 Cor. 4:3–4) and holds them captive (Heb. 2:14–15)—in order to set sinners free (John 8:36). As the apostle John explained, "The Son of God appeared for this purpose, to destroy the works of the devil" (1 John 3:8). The new King must demonstrate His power to dethrone Satan and rescue sinners from his grip. To be sure, the demons knew why the Son of God had come. They knew the King of salvation had arrived, and the prince of darkness needed his spiritual forces to do everything in their capacity to oppose Him.

From the start of the Lord's ministry, however, it was apparent that they were no match for His unsurpassed sovereign authority. It was divine power that threw them out of heaven and would one day throw them into hell. And in the middle of those two events, during Jesus' earthly ministry, the Lord's invincibility over the satanic realm was vividly put on display in every demon encounter.

This passage (1:21–28) presents one of what must have been many such encounters. Here Jesus confronts a traumatized and exposed demon while teaching in the synagogue in Capernaum. In 1:23, Mark explains that the demon cried out to Jesus. The Greek verb translated "cried out," *anakrazo*, means to scream or shout with strong emotion, and describes the shrieks of someone experiencing intense agony. The demon's screeching outcry is abrupt, disruptive, and startling. Mark relates the dark angel's panic to three aspects of Jesus' authority: the authority of His word, the authority of His judgment, and the authority of His power.

THE AUTHORITY OF HIS WORD

They went into Capernaum; and immediately on the Sabbath He entered the synagogue and began to teach. They were amazed at His teaching; for He was teaching them as one having authority, and not as the scribes. (1:21–22)

Although the demon's reaction is not recorded until verse 23, these two verses describe the initial reason for his outburst. His violent outcry came in immediate response to the authoritative teaching of Jesus. The words of Christ ignited flames of dread in his consciousness, which erupted loudly as exclamations of terror and anguish.

Mark introduced this episode by noting that they (meaning Jesus and His recently called disciples) went into Capernaum. The name Capernaum means "village of Nahum." It was likely a reference to the hometown of the Old Testament prophet Nahum. But Nahum also means "compassion," perhaps indicating that the town was also named for its compassionate residents. Located on the northwest edge of the Sea of Galilee, Capernaum was a prosperous fishing town. It was here that Peter, Andrew, James, and John had their fishing operation, and where Matthew worked as a tax collector (Matt. 9:9). Built on a major Roman road, the Via Maris, Capernaum was an important commercial town. According to historians, it had a promenade that stretched nearly a half-mile long and sat on top of an eight-foot sea wall. From there, piers jutted approximately one hundred feet out into the water, giving fishing boats easy access to the city. It contained a Roman garrison and belonged in the tetrarchy of Herod Antipas, on the border of his brother Philip's domain. After being rejected at Nazareth (Matt. 4:13; Luke 4:16–31), Jesus established His headquarters there during His Galilean ministry (cf. Mark 2:1).

Mark continued by explaining that "immediately on the Sabbath He entered the synagogue and began to teach." That was not unusual, since it had always been Jesus' habit to attend the synagogue every Sabbath (cf. Luke 4:16). The Jewish system of synagogues had initially developed in the sixth century B.C. during the Babylonian exile. Prior to the exile, worship centered in one place, the temple in Jerusalem. But when Solomon's temple was destroyed, and the Jews were in captivity for seventy years, the people began to meet together in small group gatherings. Even after the Jews returned to their homeland and rebuilt the temple, they continued to structure the community life of local villages and towns around what had become official synagogues (the Greek word translated "synagogue" means "gathering" or "assembly"). As a result, the synagogue became the center of Jewish community life—a place of local worship, a meeting hall, a school, and a courtroom. Traditionally, a synagogue could be formed in any place where there were at least ten Jewish men. Consequently, larger cities in the ancient world often contained numerous synagogues.

The Visiting Rabbi with Authority

One of the primary functions fulfilled by the synagogue was the public reading and exposition of Scripture, a practice that went back at least to the time of Nehemiah. A policy known as "freedom of the synagogue" allowed any qualified man in the congregation to deliver the exposition of the Old Testament passage. That privilege was often extended to visiting rabbis, as it was on this occasion to Jesus. Because the news about Jesus' miracles had already spread (cf. Luke 4:14), the attendees in Capernaum would have been eager to hear Him teach.

Mark does not detail the content of the message Jesus preached to the congregation that Saturday in Capernaum. Instead, he focused on the people's response. "They were amazed at His teaching; for He was teaching them as one having authority, and not as the scribes." The people were shocked. Never before had they heard a rabbi speak with such power, precision, and gravitas.

The word "authority" (*exousia*) speaks of rule, dominion, jurisdiction, full right, power, privilege, and prerogative. Jesus taught with absolute conviction, objectivity, dominion, and clarity. He spoke the truth with the unwavering confidence of the divine King, and the people could only respond in wonder (cf. Matt. 7:28–29). What a contrast Jesus' profoundly piercing words were to the esoteric pontifications of the scribes, who loved to quote the multitudinous views of other rabbis. They often taught in ways that were mystical, muddled, and often focused on minutiae. But Jesus was clearly different. He did not derive His theology from the musings of other people, nor did He offer a variety of possible explanations. His teaching was absolute, not arbitrary. It was logical and concrete, not evasive or esoteric. His arguments were reasonable, inescapable, and focused on essential matters.

Scribes were the primary teachers in first-century Jewish society. They traced their heritage back to Ezra who, according to Ezra 7:10 and Nehemiah 8:4–8, read the Law and explained it to the people. Most people had only limited access to the Scriptures, copies of which were too expensive for ordinary, working-class people to own. Consequently, they would go to the synagogue to hear the

THE DEITY OF CHRIST

Scriptures read and explained by the scribes. Because they handled the Scriptures, the scribes became so revered that they were given the title "rabbi," meaning "honored one." Over the centuries, from the time of Ezra to the time of Christ, the teaching of the scribes grew less focused on the text of Scripture, and more focused on what previous rabbis had said. By the first century, scribes prided themselves on being familiar with all possible views. Rather than faithfully explaining the simple meaning of Scripture, they delighted in complex musings, fanciful allegories, obscure insights, mystical notions, and the teachings of earlier rabbis.

So when Jesus began to explain the biblical text perfectly with clarity, conviction, and authority, His listeners were stunned. They had never heard anything like it. Their astonishment is bound up in the word "amazed" (*ekplesso*), which literally means "to be struck out of one's self" with awe and wonder. To use the vernacular, Jesus blew their minds. There are a number of New Testament words that can be translated "amazed" or "astonished." This is one of the strongest and most intense. Jesus' message was so riveting and powerful that His audience sat in stunned silence, hanging onto every word He uttered (cf. Luke 19:48).

The Violent Interruption

But the silent awe would be violently interrupted by the screams coming through the lips of a demon-possessed man. It was the demon who was panicked by the truth of Jesus' preaching and could not remain hidden in the man any longer. Mark introduces the demon in verse 23, noting the immediacy of the evil spirit's reaction to Jesus' preaching. Unable to restrain himself, the demon erupted in a fit of shrieking rage in response to the truth the Son of God proclaimed.

It is not surprising to find this evil spirit hanging around the synagogue. The demons had developed a false system of hypocritical religion that was highly successful in first-century Israel. As is their nature, demons hide in the middle of false religion, disguising themselves as angels of light (2 Cor. 11:14) and perpetuating error and deceit (cf. 1 Tim. 4:1). Like their leader Satan, they are liars and murderers who seek people's eternal destruction. In John 8:44–45, Jesus told the Pharisees, "You are of your father the devil, and you want to do the desires of your father. He was a murderer from the beginning, and does not stand in the truth because there is no truth in him. Whenever he speaks a lie, he speaks from his own nature, for he is a liar and the father of lies. But because I speak the truth, you do not believe Me."

Those verses summarize the heart of the conflict. Satan and his hosts propagate lies for the purpose of perpetuating spiritual death. But Jesus is the way, the truth, and the life (John 17:6). And when Jesus preached the truth on that Sabbath day, the demon who heard Him teach was involuntarily exposed. Confronted by the authority of Jesus' words, the fallen angel reacted with a terrified scream.

The Authority of His Judgment

Just then there was a man in their synagogue with an unclean spirit; and he cried out, saying, "What business do we have with each other, Jesus of Nazareth? Have You come to destroy us? I know who You are—the Holy One of God!" (1:23–24)

Mark's use of the phrase "just then" (*euthus*) underscores the immediacy of the demon's reaction. It followed directly on the heels of Jesus' preaching. His shrieking outburst provided audible evidence that fallen angels tremble at the power of Christ's word.

But the content of his exclamation, which is recorded in verses 23–24, indicated that the demon was also terrified by the authority of Christ's judgment.

Demon possession—always present, usually hidden—was dramatically and uniquely exposed during the ministry of Jesus Christ. The rebellious angels were unable to remain concealed in His presence. In the Old Testament there is no explicit mention of demon possession. In the book of Acts, there are only two (Acts 16:16–18; 19:13–16). The Gospels, however, abound with it (Matt. 4:24; 8:28; 9:33; 10:8; 12:22–27; Mark 1:23–27; 5:4–13; 9:25; Luke 4:41; 8:2, 28; 9:39; 13:11). Confronted by the glory of the Son of God Himself, the demons revealed their identities, often in violent and remarkable ways.

On this occasion, the demon-possessed man responded by screaming at the top of his lungs—the demon inside him borrowing the man's vocal chords to express pure terror. In a burst of dread mixed with rage, the demon asked, "What business do we have with each other, Jesus of Nazareth? Have You come to destroy us? I know who You are—the Holy One of God!"

The use of plural pronouns (*we* and *us*) suggest that this particular demon was asking these questions on behalf of fallen angels everywhere. As those who had joined in Satan's failed coup (cf. Isa. 14:12–17; Ezek. 28:12–19), demons once served in the presence of God. They knew each member of the Trinity intimately and immediately recognized Jesus as God the Son whenever they found themselves in His presence. They knew He was the Holy One of God, the messianic King who had come to save the world from the power of Satan (Luke 4:41).

In speaking to Christ, this demonic spirit employed two different names—one of which expressed his antagonism, the other his fear. The first, Jesus of Nazareth, carried a tone of scornful disdain. Nazareth was an obscure town, held in low esteem by other Israelites (cf. John 1:46). The Jewish leaders, in particular, used the term as a pejorative, because they mocked the idea that the Messiah would come from such humble, Galilean origins (cf. John 7:41, 52). In referring to Jesus' hometown, the demon joined the scorn of the disbelieving crowds.

At the same time, the evil spirit knew exactly who Jesus was. Consequently, his scorn is mixed with terrified dread. As a wretched fallen angel, his response was one of enmity intermingled with fear. He called Jesus the Holy One of God because he was fully aware of Jesus' divine authority. This unclean spirit, a being characterized by ultimate depravity and incurable wickedness, cringed in the presence of perfect virtue and holiness.

The demons knew that "the Son of God appeared for this purpose, to destroy the works of the devil" (1 John 3:8). Fully aware they were irredeemable, and would one day be cast in the lake of fire (Matt. 25:41), they feared the hour of their final destruction had come. Later in Jesus' ministry, other demons asked almost the same question: "What business do we have with each other, Son of God? Have You come here to torment us before the time?" The demons recognized exactly who Jesus was. They knew He had full authority and power to cast them into eternal punishment on God's appointed judgment day. That is why they repeatedly responded with such panic and dismay (cf. James 2:19).

The impending reality of future judgment explains the demon's response to Jesus on that Sabbath day in Capernaum. As an operative of Satan, he would have undoubtedly preferred to remain undetected—hidden in the shadows of hypocritical religion.

Instead, overwhelmed with dread and panic, he could only un-cover himself in a dramatic outburst.

The Authority of His Power

And Jesus rebuked him, saying, "Be quiet, and come out of him!" Throwing him into convulsions, the unclean spirit cried out with a loud voice and came out of him. They were all amazed, so that they debated among themselves, saying, "What is this? A new teaching with authority! He commands even the unclean spirits, and they obey Him." Immediately the news about Him spread everywhere into all the surrounding district of Galilee. (1:25–28)

Though the eschatological day of eternal judgment for Satan and his angels has not yet come (cf. Rev. 20:10), this demon was given a foretaste of Christ's absolute authority over him. He was cast out by the same power that will one day cast him into the lake of fire.

Unfazed by the demon's histrionics, Jesus rebuked him. As the divine King, He possessed the inherent authority to command this fallen angel. No dialogue, negotiation, or struggle was necessary. Attempted exorcisms involving various formulas and rituals were not uncommon among the Jews of New Testament times, though they produced no real success. But Jesus' success rate was perfect. He never failed to cast out the demons He confronted, nor did He rely on any special formulas or rituals to do so. He simply issued a command, and the demons obeyed.

The Lord delegated that power to His apostles, and they did the same (Luke 9:1). Apart from Jesus and the apostles, the New Testa-ment never presents exorcism as a practice in which believers ought to engage. In fact, when non-apostles tried to usurp that kind of authority, the results were disastrous. The seven sons of Sceva learned that lesson painfully. When they tried to cast an evil spirit out of a man by the power of "Jesus whom Paul preaches, . . . the evil spirit answered and said to them, 'I recognize Jesus, and I know about Paul, but who are you?' And the man, in whom was the evil spirit, leaped on them and subdued all of them and overpowered them, so that they fled out of that house naked and wounded" (Acts 19:13–16). Rather than engaging in exorcisms, believers today are called to engage in evangelism. Whenever we bring the gospel to non-believers and they put their faith in the Lord Jesus Christ, the Holy Spirit washes them clean, takes up residence, and the demons are evicted.

Two Powerful Commands

Jesus' rebuke came in the form of two short imperatives: "Be quiet, and come out of him!" The demon had no choice but to obey immediately. The first command silenced the demon; the second drove him out. Throughout Jesus' ministry, He repeatedly forbade the unclean spirits to testify about Him (cf. Mark 1:34). Though their identification of Jesus was accurate, He did not need nor desire any publicity from the agents of Satan. As it was, the religious leaders accused Him of casting "out demons only by Beelzebul the ruler of the demons" (Matt. 12:24). Permitting the demons to continue speaking about Him would only have added support to the sneering speculations of the Pharisees. So whenever they affirmed His identity, He shut them up (cf. Acts 16:16–19).

Jesus' second command, "come out of him," resulted in the demon's violent departure. The unclean spirit preferred to remain to hold that man's soul captive for hell. But he was forced to go, unwillingly and not quietly. As Mark records, "Throwing him into convulsions, the unclean spirit cried out with a loud voice and came out of him." With one dramatic final protest, causing the man's body to convulse, the demon let out a final scream as he departed.

The scene is reminiscent of another demon Jesus encountered, later in His ministry, the day after His transfiguration. Mark relates that story in Mark 9:25–27:

> When Jesus saw that a crowd was rapidly gathering, He rebuked the unclean spirit, saying to it, "You deaf and mute spirit, I command you, come out of him and do not enter him again." After crying out and throwing him into terrible convulsions, it came out; and the boy became so much like a corpse that most of them said, "He is dead!" But Jesus took him by the hand and raised him; and he got up.

Like the demon described in Mark 1:23, this demon showed his rebellious objection to Christ with a final, violent thrashing of his victim. But it was only a momentary frenzy. Like every other fallen angel, he was no match for the sovereign power of the divine King; and once he left, the boy whom he had tormented was healed. Though the demon-possessed man in the synagogue in Capernaum was similarly thrown into convulsions, the demon did no damage. As Luke explains in the parallel account: "When the demon had thrown him down in the midst of the people, he came out of him without doing him any harm" (Luke 4:35).

Neither Mark nor Luke provide any biographical information about the man who was delivered. But the lack of detail is intentional, because the focus is not on him. It is on the One who liberated him from demonic possession. Appropriately, the attention centers on the Son of God who again publicly displayed His divine power. By His own authority He commanded the demon to flee. Only the divine King has the power necessary to break the bondage of Satan. He can destroy the devil, dismantle his forces, and deliver captive souls.

The Reactions of the Crowd

Jesus' power was unmistakable, so that those who sat in the synagogue, who had already been amazed by His teaching, were all amazed at His ability to deliver this demon-possessed man. They had no category for what they had just witnessed, "so that they debated among themselves, saying, 'What is this? A new teaching with authority! He commands even the unclean spirits, and they obey Him.'" The crowd began to buzz with excitement over what had transpired. They had been stunned by the authority of His teaching, and then equally shocked by the power He exercised over the unclean spirits. The debate was not a formal one, but rather the excited chatter of wonder expressed by those who were amazed. Eventually, however, that debate would grow more polarizing. While no one could deny His authority over demons, the religious leaders would begin to question the source of that authority (cf. Matt. 12:24).

In the meantime, word about Jesus began to get out. As Mark explains, "Immediately the news about Him spread everywhere into all the surrounding district of Galilee." This was just the beginning. Mark 1:39 reports that "He went into their synagogues throughout all Galilee, preaching and casting out the demons." The divine King launched His public ministry by putting on displays of power over evil spirits unprecedented in Israel and the world (cf. Matt. 9:33). He taught like no one else, and He possessed and used force that no one else had ever seen. Behind His power was

Jesus' authority. The demons recognized Him and were terrified; the crowds witnessed Him and were amazed. The demons believed Him but could not be saved; the crowds refused to believe in Him and, therefore, would not be saved.

A combination of both responses is necessary for salvation. Sinners need to be both *terrified* and *amazed*: terrified by such a Judge and amazed by such a Savior. It is not enough simply to be amazed by Jesus Christ. He is not satisfied with mere curiosity, wonder, or amazement. He wants sinners to fear Him as the Judge and then run to Him as the Savior.

The people who heard Jesus teach and witnessed His authority on that Sabbath day in Capernaum were left with no excuses. Yet, the population of that city ultimately rejected Him as their Lord and Savior (Matt. 11:23; Luke 10:15). Perhaps they considered Jesus a good teacher, a moral idealist, or a misunderstood social activist. But none of those conclusions was adequate. They may have been amazed by Him in the moment, but unless they came to embrace Him in saving faith—worshiping Him as the Son of God, trusting in Him as the Savior of the world, and submitting to Him as the Lord over all—their amazement was ultimately worthless. It was no better than the trembling terror of the demons. So it is for all who reject the true person and work of Jesus Christ.

Chapter 4

CHRIST'S AUTHORITY OVER SIN AND DISEASE

MARK 2:1–12

When He had come back to Capernaum several days afterward, it was heard that He was at home. And many were gathered together, so that there was no longer room, not even near the door; and He was speaking the word to them. And they came, bringing to Him a paralytic, carried by four men. Being unable to get to Him because of the crowd, they removed the roof above Him; and when they had dug an opening, they let down the pallet on which the paralytic was lying. And Jesus seeing their faith said to the paralytic, "Son, your sins are forgiven." But some of the scribes were sitting there and reasoning in their hearts, "Why does this man speak that way? He is blaspheming; who can forgive sins but God alone?" Immediately Jesus, aware in His spirit that they were reasoning that way within themselves, said to them, "Why are you reasoning about these things in your hearts? Which is easier, to say to the paralytic, 'Your sins are forgiven'; or to say, 'Get up, and pick up your pallet and walk'? But so that you may know that the Son of Man has authority on earth to forgive sins"—He said to the paralytic, "I say to you, get up, pick up your pallet and go home." And he got up

and immediately picked up the pallet and went out in the sight of everyone, so that they were all amazed and were glorifying God, saying, "We have never seen anything like this." (2:1–12)

The most distinctive benefit that Christianity offers the world is not sacrificial love for others, a high standard of morality, or a sense of purpose and satisfaction in life. All of those virtues are by-products of biblical Christianity, but they are far from Christianity's greatest gift to humanity. The gospel offers one surpassing benefit that transcends all others and is provided by no other religion. It corresponds directly to mankind's greatest need. Only Christianity provides a permanent solution for humanity's fundamental and far-reaching problem—namely, the reality that sinners stand guilty before Holy God, who has justly condemned them to eternal hell because of their rebellion and lawlessness.

Ultimately, God does not send people to hell because of sin, but because of unforgiven sin. Hell is populated by people whose sins were never forgiven. The difference between those who look forward to eternal life in heaven and those who will experience everlasting punishment in hell is not a matter of personal goodness, as other religions teach, but is bound up entirely in one word: forgiveness. Since "all have sinned" (Rom. 3:23), both eternal destinations are inhabited by people who were sinners in this life. But only those in heaven acknowledged their sinful state and were granted divine forgiveness and the accompanying imputed righteousness that is appropriated by grace through faith in Jesus Christ (cf. Rom. 5:9, 19).

THE SOLUTION TO
MANKIND'S GREATEST PROBLEM

The Offer of Divine Forgiveness

Simply stated, every person's greatest need is the forgiveness of sin. Consequently, the greatest benefit of the gospel is its offer of divine pardon to those who believe. No other religion provides the means for full forgiveness; consequently, all other religions are actually collecting souls for hell.

Both divine judgment and divine forgiveness are consistent with God's nature. While His righteousness demands that every sin be punished (cf. Ex. 23:7; Deut. 7:10; Job 10:14; Nah. 1:3), His mercy patiently stays His wrath and makes provision for sinners to be pardoned (cf. Num. 14:18; Deut. 4:31; Ps. 86:15; 103:8–12; 108:4; 145:8; Isa. 43:25; Joel 2:13). The justice and mercy of God are repeatedly juxtaposed throughout Scripture, and there is no sense in which they represent irreconcilable truths (cf. Romans 9:14–24). In Exodus 34:6–7, God introduced Himself with these words,

> The LORD, the LORD God, compassionate and gracious, slow to anger, and abounding in lovingkindness and truth; who keeps lovingkindness for thousands, who forgives iniquity, transgression and sin; yet He will by no means leave the guilty unpunished, visiting the iniquity of fathers on the children and on the grandchildren to the third and fourth generations.

Nehemiah 9 reiterates that same refrain: "You are a God of forgiveness, gracious and compassionate, slow to anger and abounding in lovingkindness. . . . However, You are just in all that has come upon us; for You have dealt faithfully, but we have acted wickedly" (vv. 17, 33). In Romans 2:4–5, Paul emphasizes both the mercy and justice of God when he warns unbelievers what will happen if they do not repent: "Do you think lightly of the riches of His kindness and tolerance and patience, not knowing that the kindness of God leads you to repentance? But because of your stubbornness and unrepentant heart you are storing up wrath for yourself in the day of wrath and revelation of the righteous judgment of God." On the one hand, there is nothing more offensive to God's holiness than sin. Unforgiven sinners will be punished by divine wrath. On the other hand, in His mercy, God finds glory in offering to all the forgiveness and absolution of sin through the gospel.

The Satisfying of God's Justice

God can both uphold justice and forgive sinners because His justice has been satisfied by His Son, who died as a substitute for sinners (2 Cor. 5:20–21; Col. 2:13–14). Therein lies the heart of the Christian message: the Son of God became a man and died for sinners so that God's justice was satisfied and sinful men might be reconciled to God (cf. Heb. 2:14–18). The sacrifice of Christ is the sole means by which God offers forgiveness to the world (John 3:16; 14:6). The apostle Paul said it this way in Acts 13:38: "Therefore let it be known to you, brethren, that through Him forgiveness of sins is proclaimed to you and through Him everyone who believes is freed from all things." Ephesians 1:7–8 echoes those words: "In Him we have redemption through His blood, the forgiveness of our trespasses according to the riches of His grace which He lavished on us." The good news of salvation is that God eagerly forgives all who truly believe in the person and work of the Lord Jesus Christ.

The second chapter of Mark opens with a story about forgiveness. In the first chapter, Mark emphasized the divine authority of Jesus in several ways. His proclamation of the gospel was authoritative, as He called His disciples to leave everything and follow Him (1:14–20). His teaching was authoritative, such that it astonished those who heard Him (1:27). His healings were authoritative, as He displayed supernatural power over both demons and disease (1:25, 31, 34, 42). In this passage (2:1–12), Mark highlights the most necessary aspect of Jesus' divine privilege, the authority to forgive sins. That emphasis is at the heart of this unforgettable miracle.

The account centers on four different characters: the curious spectators, the crippled sinner, the compassionate Savior, and the calloused scribes. After tracking each of these, Mark concludes this account by returning to the crowd of onlookers and noting their surprise at everything they had just witnessed.

The Curious Spectators

When He had come back to Capernaum several days afterward, it was heard that He was at home. And many were gathered together, so that there was no longer room, not even near the door; and He was speaking the word to them. (2:1–2)

Earlier, when Jesus left Capernaum, He went to preach the gospel in the surrounding towns and villages (1:38). But after He healed the man with leprosy, the word about Him spread to such an extent that He "could no longer publicly enter a city, but stayed out in unpopulated areas; and they were coming to Him from everywhere" (1:45). Mark's comment that it was several days afterward is a very broad phrase that encompasses an indefinite period of time (cf. Luke 5:17). However long it had been (possibly weeks or even months), when Jesus came back to Capernaum, He must have done so quietly. The need for a discreet entrance into Capernaum is indicated by Mark 1:45. It was not long, however, before "it was heard that He was at home." Though He had come back secretly, His presence became very public and eager crowds began to gather. The reference to Jesus' home was in keeping with His decision to make Capernaum His base of operations during His Galilean ministry. While in Capernaum, He likely stayed at the house of Peter and Andrew (cf. 1:29).

The last time He had been at Peter's home, the residents of Capernaum gathered en masse outside the house as Jesus healed all the sick who were brought to Him (1:33–34). As usual, on this occasion word spread that Jesus was there and a crowd immediately began to form. Mark's comment that "many were gathered together" is an understatement. People were crammed in so tightly that "there was no longer room, not even near the door."

The Onlookers and Miracle Seekers

As always, the crowds primarily consisted of inquisitive onlookers and miracle seekers (Matt. 16:4), more interested in pursuing their own desires (John 6:26) than in mourning over and repenting from sin, thereby seeking salvation from Christ. There were, of course, some genuine followers and true believers, but they represented a small minority. For the most part, the multitudes remained spiritually indifferent to Jesus—drawn by their curiosity and fascination with His supernatural works, but ultimately unwilling to embrace His saving words (Mark 8:34–38; John 6:66). Despite such spiritual apathy and ambivalence, the Lord continued to preach to the throngs, knowing that the Father would draw out the elect from among them (John 6:37, 44). On this occasion in the house in Capernaum, as was His custom, "He was speaking the word to them."

The Pharisees and Scribes

The crowd included a number of Pharisees (Luke 5:17), who were the primary guardians and advocates of the legalistic traditions and rituals that permeated first-century Judaism. The name "Pharisee," meaning "separated one," defined the philosophy behind the movement. Those who joined the sect, which numbered around six thousand, diligently avoided any interaction with Gentiles, tax collectors, or people whom they regarded as "sinners" (cf. Luke 7:39). Even their attitude toward the common Jewish people was one of disdain and condescension (cf. John 7:49). They considered themselves to be the most holy of all Israelites, but their "holiness" was entirely external and superficial (cf. Matt. 23:28). It mainly consisted of adherence to their own man-made rules and regulations—stipulations they had added through the years to the law of Moses (cf. Matt. 15:2–9).

The precise origin of the Pharisees is not known. But it is likely that their sect formed sometime before the middle of the second century B.C. By the time of Jesus' ministry, they comprised the dominant religious group in Israel. Fervently devoted to keeping the people loyal to both the Old Testament law, and more importantly, the complex set of extrabiblical traditions they had developed around the Law, they were highly esteemed for their apparent spirituality and scriptural fidelity.

Within the sect there were scribes (2:6, 16), also referred to as "lawyers" (cf. Luke 10:25), who were professional theologians and Old Testament scholars. They traced their history back to the time of Ezra and Nehemiah, when the Israelites returned to their homeland after the Babylonian captivity. An ancient Jewish tradition asserted that God gave the Law to angels, who gave it to Moses and Joshua, who gave it to the elders, who gave it to the prophets, who gave it to the scribes in order to lead and teach in the synagogues. The scribes were responsible both to copy and preserve the Scriptures, as well as interpret them in order to instruct the people. Because there were no more Old Testament prophets after Malachi, the scribes fulfilled the foundational teaching role in Israel. Scribes could be found in various Jewish sects (such as the Sadducees or Essenes), but most scribes in Jesus' day were associated with the Pharisees.

Though a few Pharisees would come to believe in Jesus (cf. John 19:39; Acts 15:5), collectively they appear openly opposed to Him. The scribes and Pharisees who intermingled in the crowd this day were not there to support Jesus' ministry or learn from Him. Rather, they were present because they saw Jesus as a growing threat. Most of them were not even from Capernaum, but from other cities around Galilee and even from Jerusalem (Luke 5:17). They had embedded themselves in the crowd of curious spectators to hear what Jesus had to say for the sole purpose of finding fault with Him, in order to discredit—and eventually eliminate—Him.

THE CRIPPLED SINNER

And they came, bringing to Him a paralytic, carried by four men. Being unable to get to Him because of the crowd, they removed the roof above Him; and when they had dug an opening, they let down the pallet on which the paralytic was lying. (2:3–4)

The account moves from the crowd of curious spectators to focus on a paralytic, carried by four men. His condition had made him completely dependent on others. Unlike lepers (cf. 1:40–45), those who suffered from paralysis were not shunned by Israelite society since their condition was not contagious. Nonetheless, because disease and disability in general were assumed to be the immediate consequence of sin (cf. John 9:2), this man was likely stigmatized by many in his community.

According to Matthew 4:24, Jesus healed many who suffered from paralysis. Yet, all three Synoptic Gospels draw attention to this particular man (cf. Matt. 9:1–8; Luke 5:17–26). His story is noteworthy not only because of the undaunted determination displayed by him and his friends to get to Jesus, but more importantly because of what Jesus did for him beyond healing his body.

Upon arrival, the five were confronted with an overflowing throng of people so tightly packed in and around the house that they were unable to get to Jesus because of the crowd. According to Luke 5:18, the four friends made an unsuccessful effort to get in through the door. Refusing to give up, they devised an aggressive and extreme plan for reaching Jesus. As Luke explains, "Not finding any way to bring him in because of the crowd, they went up on the roof" (5:19). Once there, "they removed the roof above [Jesus]; and when they had dug an opening, they let down the pallet on which the paralytic was lying" (Mark 2:4).

Jewish houses were typically one story with a flat patio roof accessible by an external staircase. The typical roof was constructed using large wooden beams with smaller pieces of wood in between, covered by a thatch consisting of grain, twigs, straw, and mud. Tiles would then be installed on top of the thatch. The four men carried their friend around the crowd and up the stairs to the roof. After determining where Jesus was located in the room below, they began removing the roof—tiles, mud, and thatch—in their effort to create an opening large enough to lower the pallet.

The strategy was effective, though it must have been incredibly disruptive. Jesus was, no doubt, teaching in the large central room of the house with people pressed around Him, when debris suddenly started falling from the ceiling onto the heads below. One can easily imagine the shock and dismay as the opening grew bigger and bigger, until it was finally large enough to lower the stretcher. Carefully, "they let down the pallet on which the paralytic was lying." According to Luke 5:19, the four men had calculated well because their friend came down directly in front of Jesus.

THE COMPASSIONATE SAVIOR

And Jesus seeing their faith said to the paralytic, "Son, your sins are forgiven." (2:5)

As the man was lowered in front of Jesus and the stunned onlookers, the reason for the gaping hole in the ceiling became obvious—the man had been brought in order to be healed. Everyone else in the room could see the man's physical need, but only Jesus perceived the deeper, more significant problem—the paralytic's need for forgiveness. Obviously, the man wanted physical restoration. But Jesus knew he longed for more than that; He addressed the more serious issue first. His words to the paralytic must have stunned everyone in the room. Seeing the faith of both the desperate man and his friends, "Jesus said to the paralytic, 'Son, your sins are forgiven.'" As shocking as the man's dramatic entrance through the roof had been, Jesus' statement was even more astonishing.

Sinful mankind has no greater need than forgiveness. It is the only means for reconciliation to God, bringing blessing in this life and eternal life in the next. The reason Jesus came is so that He might "save His people from their sins" (Matt. 1:21), and that through Him sinners might be reconciled to God (2 Cor. 5:18–19). As Peter told Cornelius, speaking of Jesus, "Of Him all the prophets bear witness that through His name everyone who believes in Him receives forgiveness of sins" (Acts 10:43; cf. 5:31; 26:18; Eph. 1:7; 4:32; Col. 1:14; 2:13–14; 3:13; 1 John 1:9; 2:12; Rev. 1:5). Divine forgiveness, by grace alone apart from works, is distinctive to the Christian gospel. It distinguishes the true message of salvation from every false system of self-righteousness and merit-based religion.

The statement "seeing their faith" seems to indicate more than just a belief in Jesus' ability to heal (cf. John 2:23–24). The forgiveness that the Lord granted indicates a genuine, repentant faith. This man (along with his friends) must have believed that Jesus was the One who offered salvation to those who repent (1:15). The Lord, recognizing his true faith, said to him, "Son, your sins are forgiven." The crippled man saw himself as a guilty sinner, spiritually disabled and in need of forgiveness, like the penitent tax collector in Luke 18:13–14 who cried out, "God, be merciful to me, the sinner!" And like the tax collector of Luke 18, this man went home justified. Through faith in Christ, he received forgiveness. The same is true for every sinner who believes. Salvation is received by grace through faith in Christ (John 14:6; Acts 4:12; 17:30–31; Rom. 3:26; 1 Tim. 2:5).

Recognizing the man's genuine faith and desire for salvation, Jesus compassionately and authoritatively forgave him of his sin. The Greek word rendered "are forgiven" refers to the idea of sending or driving away (Ps. 103:12; Jer. 31:34; Mic. 7:19). Complete pardon was granted by divine grace, apart from any merit or works-righteousness on the part of the paralyzed man. Jesus obliterated his guilt and, in that very moment, the crippled sinner was delivered from a future in everlasting hell to one in eternal heaven.

THE CALLOUSED SCRIBES

But some of the scribes were sitting there and reasoning in their hearts, "Why does this man speak that way? He is blaspheming; who can forgive sins but God alone?" Immediately Jesus, aware in His spirit that they were reasoning that way within themselves, said to them, "Why are you reasoning about these things in your hearts? Which is easier, to say to the paralytic, 'Your sins are forgiven'; or to say, 'Get up, and pick up your pallet and walk'? But so that you may know that the Son of Man has authority on earth to forgive sins"—He said to the paralytic, "I say to you, get up, pick up your pallet and go home." (2:6–11)

Jesus' declaration of forgiveness gave the hostile religious leaders all the ammunition they were looking for to attack Him. When they heard what Jesus said, "some of the scribes were sitting there and reasoning in their hearts, 'Why does this man speak that way? He is blaspheming; who can forgive sins but God alone?'"

The Charge of Blasphemy

Their premise, that only God can grant full forgiveness of sins, is absolutely correct. The justification of sinners is a prerogative that belongs to God alone. As the supreme Judge, only He can grant eternal pardon to wicked people. And since every sin is ultimately an act of rebellion against Him and His law (Ps. 51:4), the right to forgive, as well as the right to condemn, belongs to God alone.

Because He claimed a level of authority that belongs only to God (cf. Matt. 26:65; John 10:33), the scribes saw Jesus as a blasphemer. From the perspective of the Jews, blasphemy was the most horrendous crime a person could commit. The first-century Jews identified three levels of blasphemy. First, a person was charged with blasphemy if he spoke evil of the law of God. Stephen (Acts 6:13) and Paul (Acts 21:27–28) were each wrongly accused of doing this. A second, more serious, type of blasphemy occurred when a person spoke evil of God directly (cf. Ex. 20:7). Cursing the name of the Lord, for example, was a crime punishable by death (Lev. 24:10–16). A third form of blasphemy, even more heinous than the other two, took place when a sinful human being claimed to possess divine authority and equality with God. For a mere mortal to act as if he were God was the most egregious offense of all. It was this form of blasphemy that the Jewish religious leaders charged Jesus with committing (cf. John 5:18; 8:58–59; 10:33).

Eventually, they would use these same accusations to justify His murder (John 19:7; cf. Lev. 24:23).

Three Displays of Christ's Deity

In the face of their allegations of blasphemy, Jesus demonstrated His deity in three important ways. *First, He read their minds.* As Mark explains, "Immediately Jesus [was] aware in His spirit that they were reasoning that way within themselves." The fact that He knew their thoughts proved His deity, since only God is omniscient (1 Sam. 16:7; 1 Kings 8:39; 1 Chron. 28:9; Jer. 17:10; Ezek. 11:5). Jesus did not need them to verbalize their thoughts, "for He Himself knew what was in man" (John 2:25).

Second, He did not argue against their basic theological premise, that only God can forgive sins. Rather, He affirmed that truth. Jesus knew that the religious leaders were accusing Him of the blasphemy of claiming equality with God. That was His whole point. *His claim to be able to forgive sins was nothing less than a claim that He was God.*

Third, He backed up His claim by demonstrating divine power. Having unmasked their thoughts, Jesus said to them, "Why are you reasoning about these things in your hearts? Which is easier, to say to the paralytic, 'Your sins are forgiven'; or to say, 'Get up, and pick up your pallet and walk'?" Jesus was not asking which is easier to do, since both are beyond human ability. Rather, He was asking which is easier to claim as a convincing reality. Obviously, it is easier to say that someone's sins are forgiven since there is no empirical way to confirm or deny the reality of that claim. Conversely, telling a paralyzed man to get up and walk is something that can be immediately tested.

Jesus purposely waited to heal the paralyzed man until after He declared His authority to forgive sins. Disease and disability are consequences of living in a fallen world, meaning that sin's permeating effects are the root cause of all sickness and suffering. By healing the paralyzed man, in demonstration of His power over sin's effects, Jesus proved His authority over sin itself. The Lord thus performed the undeniable miracle of physical healing so that everyone watching would "know that the Son of Man has authority on earth to forgive sins." The title Son of Man was one of Jesus' favorite self-designations. He used it more than eighty times in the Gospels (with fourteen of those occurrences in the book of Mark). Not only did the title humbly identify His humanity, but it also had messianic implications (cf. Daniel 7:13, 14).

Looking with compassion at the man still lying on the stretcher, Jesus said to him, "I say to you, get up, pick up your pallet and go home." This miracle would prove whether or not Jesus had power over sin and its effects. More to the point, it would demonstrate whether He truly had the divine authority He claimed to possess. The scribes accused Jesus of being a blasphemer. But blasphemers are not able to read minds. They cannot forgive sins. And they cannot validate their claims by healing people who are paralyzed. By performing this miracle, Jesus proved for all to see that He was not a blasphemer. And if He was not a blasphemer, then He was God as He claimed.

THE CROWD'S SURPRISE

And he got up and immediately picked up the pallet and went out in the sight of everyone, so that they were all amazed and were glorifying God, saying, "We have never seen anything like this." (2:12)

Jesus dramatically put His lofty claims to the test by telling the paralyzed man to get up and walk. Verification came instantly. The man "got up and immediately picked up the pallet and went out in the sight of everyone." Whenever Jesus healed anyone, the person experienced a complete and immediate recovery. No recuperation period was needed, nor were there any lingering effects of the infirmity. This man was no exception. The moment the words left Jesus' mouth, the man regained feeling, function, and full strength in every part of his body. He did not need months of physical therapy to relearn how to stand or walk. Instead, he stood right up, picked up his stretcher, and walked home. This time the crowd, utterly amazed by all that had just transpired, parted to let him pass. According to Luke 5:25, the former cripple went home "glorifying God" that not only had his body been healed, but his sins had been forgiven.

Unlike the calloused scribes and Pharisees, who continued to reject Christ in spite of the undeniable signs He performed (cf. Luke 6:11; 11:15, 53; 13:17; 15:1–2; 19:47; John 5:36; 10:37–38), the crowds responded with surprise and astonishment. As Mark explains, "They were all amazed and were glorifying God, saying, 'We have never seen anything like this.'" The Greek word for "amazed" means to be astonished, confused, or even to lose one's mind. The people were absolutely dumbfounded by what they had just seen. Luke adds, "They were filled with fear, saying, 'We have seen remarkable things today'" (Luke 5:26). The word Luke uses for "fear" is *phobos* which, in this context, describes the awestruck reverence that comes from being exposed to the person, presence, and power of God (cf. Luke 1:12, 65; 2:9; 7:16; 8:37; 21:26; Matt. 14:26; 28:4, 8; Mark 4:41; Acts 2:43; 5:5, 11; 9:31; 19:17). They responded by glorifying God, surely by offering familiar expressions of praise.

But for most in the crowd, this response was still reflective of a superficial faith. Matthew 9:8 records their reaction to this very miracle with these words, "But when the crowds saw this, they were awestruck, and glorified God, who had given such authority to men." Though they were awestruck, and though they glorified God, they still viewed Jesus a just a man to whom God had granted authority. In spite of the obvious miracle and the unprecedented demonstration of divine power, many remained unconvinced of Christ's deity. They witnessed His supernatural works, but they refused to believe in His divinity. As John explained, "But though He had performed so many signs before them, yet they were not believing in Him" (John 12:37; cf. 1 Cor. 1:22).

Jesus' miracles functioned as signs validating His claim that He possessed divine authority to forgive sinners. Moreover, Jesus not only had the power to forgive sinners, but He also would become the perfect sacrifice on which divine forgiveness is based. The words Jesus spoke to that paralyzed man two millennia ago, are the same words He still speaks to all who come to Him in genuine faith: "Your sins are forgiven." The greatest benefit Christianity offers to the world is the forgiveness of sins. Jesus Christ made forgiveness possible through His death on the cross. He offers that forgiveness to all who are willing to repent of their sin and believe in His name (cf. Rom. 10:9–10).

Chapter 5

---∞---

CHRIST'S AUTHORITY OVER THE SABBATH

MARK 2:23–28

And it happened that He was passing through the grainfields on the Sabbath, and His disciples began to make their way along while picking the heads of grain. The Pharisees were saying to Him, "Look, why are they doing what is not lawful on the Sabbath?" And He said to them, "Have you never read what David did when he was in need and he and his companions became hungry; how he entered the house of God in the time of Abiathar the high priest, and ate the consecrated bread, which is not lawful for anyone to eat except the priests, and he also gave it to those who were with him?" Jesus said to them, "The Sabbath was made for man, and not man for the Sabbath. So the Son of Man is Lord even of the Sabbath." (2:23–28)

The biblical gospels are more than just historical accounts of the earthly life of the Lord Jesus. They are also Christological treatises revealing the transcendence of His heavenly character. Written under the inspiration of the Holy Spirit, the four histories represent the perfect blending of biography and theology—a masterful combination of factual precision and doctrinal depth. Not only do they recount the story of Jesus' life and ministry with absolute accuracy, but they also simultaneously present the infinite glories of His divine person, so that their readers may come to know Him for who He really is: the Son of Man and the Son of God.

Like the other three writers, Mark's purpose was to reveal and declare the truth about the person and work of the Lord Jesus. He began his gospel by declaring Jesus to be the divine messianic King, introducing Him with a royal title: "Christ, the Son of God" (1:1). In the verses that follow, Jesus is identified as "the LORD" (1:3), the coming One (1:7), the One who baptizes with the Holy Spirit (1:8), the "beloved Son" of the Father (1:11), the One who offers the gospel of the kingdom (1:14), and "the Holy One of God" (1:24).

By chapter two, it is clear that Jesus possessed the sovereign power to authenticate such elevated titles as He demonstrated unsurpassed authority over Satan and temptation (1:12–13), demons and demon-possession (1:25–26), sickness and disease (1:29–34), sin and its effects (2:5–12), and even the social stigmas of first-century Judaism (2:13–17). His works convincingly validated His words, proving beyond any legitimate doubt that He was the Son of God, worthy of every elevated title and glorious superlative that could ever be bestowed on Him (cf. John 10:37–38). Moreover, the Old Testament had declared truth that the Messiah would be divine (cf. Pss. 2:7–12; 110:1; Prov. 30:4; Dan. 7:13–14; Jer. 23:5–6; Mic. 5:2). Isaiah 9:6 asserts His deity without qualification: "For a child will be born to us, a son will be given to us; And the government will rest on His shoulders; And His name will be called Wonderful Counselor, Mighty God, Eternal Father, Prince of Peace." Those titles find their perfect fulfillment in Jesus Christ.

The Lord of the Sabbath

In Mark 2:23–28, we are introduced to another of His titles: "Lord of the Sabbath" (v. 28). That designation, coming from Jesus' own lips, underscored His divine authority while again setting Him in direct conflict with the hypocritical religious leaders of Judaism. Conflict was inevitable whenever Jesus interacted with the Pharisees and scribes. He embodied the truth (John 14:6); they represented a system of superficial pretense and false religion. In the same way that light pierces the darkness, Christ's words illuminated Israel's corrupt religious establishment—disclosing the dead traditionalism that characterized its most ardent defenders. Jesus refused to mince words, exposing the Pharisees and scribes for who they really were: spiritually blind false teachers who turned their disciples into sons of hell (cf. Matt. 7:15–20; 15:14; 23:15). The Lord's dogmatic declarations left no room for ambiguity or ambivalence. Would His hearers remain trapped as slaves to a system of extrabiblical rules and regulations or be set free by the gospel of grace through faith in the Savior (cf. John 8:31–36)?

When Jesus declared Himself to be the Lord of the Sabbath, He struck a severe blow at the entire system of merit and works righteousness that found its focal point in the Sabbath. The seventh day of every week had become the platform for showcasing Pharisaic legalism. The command to observe the Sabbath, like the other nine commandments, was intended to promote love toward God and other people (cf. Ex. 20:1–17; Mark 12:28–31). What God established as a day of reverence toward Him and refreshment from work, the Pharisees and scribes transformed into a day of stifling regulation and restriction. Just as Jesus confronted the Sadducees for making the temple a den of robbers (Matt. 21:13), He blasted the Pharisees for turning a day of weekly worship into a rigorous burden of extraneous rule-keeping. By openly defying the man-made traditions regarding the Sabbath, Jesus put Himself in direct conflict with the religious leaders at their most sensitive point.

The religious leaders viewed Jesus as a serious threat to their religious system. He, conversely, rebuked them for being imposters. With righteous indignation, He condemned them for perpetuating a burdensome system of external ritualism. They considered themselves holy; He called them hypocrites (cf. Matt. 23). But rather than repenting, they hardened their hearts against Him. The more Jesus preached, the deeper their resentment toward Him grew. The fact that He openly associated with the outcasts of society, even calling a tax collector to be one of His closest disciples (2:14), only added to the tension. They mockingly called Him the friend of sinners (Matt. 11:19; Luke 7:34). He embraced the title, reminding them that He "did not come to call the righteous, but sinners" to repentance (Mark 2:17).

By claiming to be the Lord of the Sabbath, Jesus essentially declared His authority over the whole of Jewish religion, because Sabbath-day observance was its high point.

The implications of Christ's claim struck deeply. The pattern for a day of rest was established at creation, when God Himself rested on the seventh day (Gen. 2:2). Furthermore, it was God who wrote in the tablets of stone in Exodus 20:8, "Remember the sabbath day, to keep it holy" (cf. Ex. 31:12–17; Deut. 5:12–15). God was the One who established the Sabbath. Thus, to claim to be the Lord of the Sabbath was to claim deity, a reality that was certainly not lost on the Pharisees and scribes, who became incensed by what they perceived to be blasphemy.

John 5:1–8 recounts an event that occurred in Judea shortly

before the events recorded in Mark 2:23–28.[1] On that occasion, which took place on a Sabbath day, Jesus healed a man who had been severely ill for thirty-eight years. The Pharisees, rather than responding with compassion, were outraged because Jesus told the man to pick up his bed mat and walk home—an act that violated rabbinic regulations for the Sabbath. As John explains,

> Immediately the man became well, and picked up his pallet and began to walk. Now it was the Sabbath on that day. So the Jews were saying to the man who was cured, "It is the Sabbath, and it is not permissible for you to carry your pallet." But he answered them, "He who made me well was the one who said to me, 'Pick up your pallet and walk.'" They asked him, "Who is the man who said to you, 'Pick up your pallet and walk'?" But the man who was healed did not know who it was, for Jesus had slipped away while there was a crowd in that place. Afterward Jesus found him in the temple and said to him, "Behold, you have become well; do not sin anymore, so that nothing worse happens to you." The man went away, and told the Jews that it was Jesus who had made him well. For this reason the Jews were persecuting Jesus, because He was doing these things on the Sabbath. But He answered them, "My Father is working until now, and I Myself am working." For this reason therefore the Jews were seeking all the more to kill Him, because He not only was breaking the Sabbath, but also was calling God His own Father, making Himself equal with God. (John 5:9–18)

Man-Made Regulations for the Sabbath

The Jewish religious leaders hated Jesus because He violated their man-made Sabbath regulations. But they detested Him all the more because, in the process of ignoring their extrabiblical rules, He claimed equality with God. When Jesus designated Himself the Lord of the Sabbath, He was not getting sidetracked with peripheral issues. With that single claim, Jesus directly assaulted apostate Judaism while simultaneously declaring His divinity. He called Israel to return to the true purpose of the Sabbath—the purpose He Himself had established for it when He issued the fourth commandment to Moses centuries earlier (cf. John 5:46; 8:58).

The Sabbath was intended to be a day of worship and rest for God's people under the Old Covenant. The word "sabbath" itself is derived from the Hebrew term *shabbat* meaning "to rest," "to cease," or "to desist." On the seventh day of each week, the Israelites were to refrain from working in order to focus their attention on honoring the Lord. Over the ensuing fifteen centuries, from the time of Moses to the ministry of Jesus, the Sabbath accumulated a vast number of additional rabbinic rules and restrictions, which made observing the seventh day an overpowering burden (cf. Matt. 15:6, 9). No less than twenty-four chapters of the Talmud (the central text of rabbinic Judaism) focus on Sabbath regulations, meticulously detailing the almost innumerable specifics of what constituted acceptable behavior.

Almost no area of life was spared from the fastidious Sabbath regulations of the rabbis, which were designed to gain God's favor. There were laws about wine, honey, milk, spitting, writing, and getting dirt off of clothes. Anything that might be contrived as work was forbidden. Thus, on a Sabbath, scribes could not carry their pens, tailors their needles, or students their books. To do so might tempt them to work on the Sabbath. For that matter, carrying anything heavier than a dried fig was forbidden; and if the object in question had been picked up in a public place it could only be set down in a private place. If the object were tossed into the air, it had to be caught with the same hand. To catch it with the other hand would constitute work, and therefore be a violation of the Sabbath. No insects could be killed. No candle or flame could be lit or extinguished. Nothing could be bought or sold. No bathing was allowed, since water might spill onto the floor and accidentally wash it. No furniture could be moved inside the house, since it might create ruts in the dirt floor and thereby constitute plowing. An egg could not be boiled even if all one did was place it in the hot desert sand. A radish could not be left in salt because it would become a pickle, and pickling constituted work.

On the Sabbath, sick people were only allowed enough treatment to keep them alive. Any medical treatment that improved their condition was considered work, and therefore prohibited. It was not even permissible for women to look in a mirror, since they might be tempted to pull out any gray hairs they spotted. Nor were they allowed to wear jewelry, since jewelry weighs more than a dried fig.

Other activities that were banned on the Sabbath included washing clothes, dyeing wool, shearing sheep, spinning wool, tying or untying a knot, sowing seed, plowing a field, reaping a harvest, binding sheaves, threshing wheat, grinding flour, kneading dough, hunting a deer, or preparing its meat. One of the more interesting restrictions related to the distance people could travel on the Sabbath. A person was not allowed to travel more than 3,000 feet from home (or to take more than 999 steps). But, due to practical concerns, the rabbis devised creative ways to get around this. If one placed food at the 3,000 foot point before the Sabbath began, that point was considered an extension of one's home, thereby enabling a person to travel another 3,000 feet. Or, if a rope or piece of wood was placed across a narrow street or alley, it was considered a door-way—making it part of one's home and allowing the 3,000 feet of travel to begin there. Even in modern times, Jewish neighbor-hoods connect houses together using cords and ropes (known as an "eruv"). Doing so, from the perspective of rabbinic law, creates a single home out of every connected building—allowing people to move freely within the defined area without being limited to the 3,000-foot restriction, and to carry certain household items like keys, medicine, strollers, canes, and babies.[2]

The man-made traditions perpetuated by the Pharisees and scribes clearly placed a crushing weight on the people (cf. Matt. 15:3; 23:4; Luke 11:46; Acts 15:10). In contrast, Jesus welcomed His hearers with liberating words of true refreshment: "Come to Me, all who are weary and heavy-laden, and I will give you rest. Take My yoke upon you and learn from Me, for I am gentle and humble in heart, and you will find rest for your souls. For My yoke is easy and My burden is light" (Matt. 11:28–30). The Lord was not talking about relieving physical labor. Rather, He was offering freedom to those under the burden of an oppressive, sabbatarian legalism from which they could get no relief and which could not gain them salvation

As a side note, it is important to understand that observing the Sabbath is not required of believers in the church age (Col. 2:16; cf. Rom. 14:5–6; Gal. 4:9–10). The early church set aside Sunday, the first day of the week, as the day on which it gathered for worship, in-struction, and fellowship (cf. Acts 20:7; 1 Cor. 16:2). However, it is not accurate to equate the "Lord's Day" (Sunday) with the Old Tes-tament Sabbath, since the New Testament abrogates the Sabbath completely. Still this instruction by our Lord regarding that day (in Mark 2:23–28) contains rich christological truths for the church.

In this passage, Mark records the first of two incidents in which Christ directly challenged the Pharisees' false understanding of the Sabbath. The second incident (recorded in Mark 3:1–6) took place in the synagogue. This incident (2:23–28), which probably happened one week earlier as Jesus and His disciples were walking through some grain fields, can be understood under four headings: the Sabbath incident (v. 23), the scornful indictment (v. 24), the scriptural illustration (vv. 25–26), and the sovereign interpreter (vv. 27–28).

THE SABBATH INCIDENT

And it happened that He was passing through the grainfields on the Sabbath, and His disciples began to make their way along while picking the heads of grain. (v. 23)

On this particular Sabbath, Jesus and His disciples were walking through fields where grain was growing. The Pharisees were dogging His steps carefully. As "He was passing through the grainfields on the Sabbath," some of His disciples became hungry (Matt. 12:1). And so, "they began to make their way along while picking the heads of grain." Luke adds that they were "rubbing them in their hands, and eating the grain" (Luke 6:1). The crop being grown in these particular fields was probably wheat or barley. In Israel, grain ripens from April to August, indicating that this event likely took place in spring or summer.

In the ancient world, it was normal for pathways to crisscross fields, so travelers traversed through crops routinely. Roads were scarce, especially in rural places, so travel usually took place on wide paths that stretched from one town to the next, passing through fields and pastures. As they journeyed on their way, people walked alongside the crops that lined both sides of the path. In light of this, God had prescribed a provision for His people. According to Deuteronomy 23:25, "When you enter your neighbor's standing grain, then you may pluck the heads with your hand, but you shall not wield a sickle in your neighbor's standing grain." To harvest someone else's grain (with a sickle) was not permitted for obvious reasons. But to pluck a few heads of grain while walking beside a ripened field of wheat or barley was a provision made by God Himself.

Jesus' disciples were doing exactly what the Old Testament permitted them to do. When they picked off the heads of grain, rubbed the heads in their hands to remove the husk and shell, and then ate the kernel, their actions were perfectly allowable within the purposes of God, but not in the minds of religious Jews.

THE SCORNFUL INDICTMENT

The Pharisees were saying to Him, "Look, why are they doing what is not lawful on the Sabbath?" (v. 24)

It is hard to imagine how the Pharisees could have followed Jesus through the grain fields while staying within 3,000 feet of their homes. Whatever the justification for their own transgressions, they observed Jesus' disciples violating rabbinic law and became incensed. They charged the disciples with doing what is not lawful. But as noted, Jesus and His followers had not transgressed any biblical law. The Pharisees had elevated their own man-made tradition over Scripture (cf. Matt. 15:3, 6). They established themselves as the authority over Sabbath-day observances, usurping the rightful position of the only true Lord of the Sabbath—as Jesus would soon make clear.

When the Pharisees saw what the disciples were doing, they

were outraged. Offended that Jesus would allow His followers to commit such a blatant violation, they said to Him, "Look, why are they doing what is not lawful to do on the Sabbath?" According to Luke 6:2, they did not limit their attack only to the disciples, but targeted Jesus as well. The only law being transgressed was that of the Pharisees. But by rabbinic standards, the disciples were guilty of several forbidden actions: reaping (by picking the grain), sifting (by removing the husks and shell), threshing (by rubbing the heads of grain), winnowing (by throwing the chaff in the air), and preparing a meal (by eating the grain after they had cleaned it). None of those activities were permitted on the Sabbath.

Not concerned about the hunger or well-being of Jesus' disciples, the Pharisees' only interest was in protecting the petty regulations that made up their hypocritical system of external religion. They followed Jesus to scrutinize His behavior, solely to find something for which to indict Him. The heart attitude behind their question was one of hatred toward Jesus, because He and His followers lived in such open defiance to their system of religion, in which the Sabbath was central.

THE SCRIPTURAL ILLUSTRATION

And He said to them, "Have you never read what David did when he was in need and he and his companions became hungry; how he entered the house of God in the time of Abiathar the high priest, and ate the consecrated bread, which is not lawful for anyone to eat except the priests, and he also gave it to those who were with him?" (vv. 25–26)

Without any apology, Jesus responded by challenging their authority and exposing their ignorance of the Old Testament. He said to them, "Have you never read what David did when he was in need and he and his companions became hungry; how he entered the house of God in the time of Abiathar the high priest, and ate the consecrated bread, which is not lawful for anyone to eat except the priests, and he also gave it to those who were with him?" Obviously, the Pharisees had read the story about David. But Jesus' words highlighted the fact that, even though they knew the facts of the story, they were ignorant of its true meaning. Thus, He responded to their question with one of His own: "Have you never read?" The rhetorical question exposed the inexcusable ignorance of those who were the self-proclaimed experts on Scripture and the teachers of Israel (cf. Matt. 19:4; 21:42; 22:31; Mark 12:10; John 3:10). In effect, Jesus was asking them, "If you are such fastidious students of Scripture, why don't you know what it says?"

The account to which Jesus referred is found in 1 Samuel 21:1–6. David, fleeing empty-handed to Gibeah to escape Saul, came to the tabernacle which was located at Nob, about a mile north of Jerusalem. Hungry and without proper provisions, David asked Ahimelech, the priest, for food.

> The priest answered David and said, "There is no ordinary bread on hand, but there is consecrated bread; if only the young men have kept themselves from women." David answered the priest and said to him, "Surely women have been kept from us as previously when I set out and the vessels of the young men were holy, though it was an ordinary journey; how much more then today will their vessels be holy?" So the priest gave him consecrated bread; for there was no bread there but the bread of the Presence which was removed from before the Lord, in order to put hot bread in its place when it was taken away. (1 Sam. 21:4–6)

The only bread at the tabernacle was "the bread of the Presence" (Ex. 25:30). Every Sabbath, twelve loaves of consecrated bread were baked and set on the gold table in the Holy Place. After the fresh loaves were placed, the priests were allowed to eat the week-old bread, but no one else was permitted to eat it (Lev. 24:9). Recognizing their need, Ahimelech showed compassion to David and his men by making an exception and giving them the consecrated bread. His only condition was that "the young men [must] have kept themselves from women" so that they would be ceremonially clean. Significantly, God did not punish either Ahimelech or David for their actions. He allowed a ceremonial law to be violated for the sake of meeting an urgent human need. In fact, the only person offended by Ahimelech's act of kindness was the volatile King Saul (1 Sam. 22:11–18).

Jesus' point, as illustrated by the Old Testament account, was that showing compassion, in God's sight, always trumped strict adherence to ritual and ceremony. His illustration employed the familiar rabbinic style of arguing from the lesser to the greater. If it was permissible for Ahimelech, a human priest, to make an exception to God's ceremonial law in order to aid David and his men, it was surely appropriate for the Son of God to disregard unbiblical rabbinic tradition in order to meet the needs of His disciples. But the religious leaders were far more concerned with preserving their own authority than with the needs of anyone else. And, in a similar way to Saul's pursuit of David to kill him, the Pharisees were already seeking to put the Son of David to death.

According to Matthew's account (12:5–6), Jesus also told the Pharisees, "Or have you not read in the Law, that on the Sabbath the priests in the temple break the Sabbath and are innocent? But I say to you that something greater than the temple is here."

By pointing to the example of the priests, Jesus demonstrated the inconsistency of the Pharisees' own legalistic standard. Each Sabbath, the ministering priests were required to light fires for the altar and slaughter animals for sacrifice (cf. Num. 28:9–10; cf. Lev. 24:8–9). These activities clearly violated the rabbinic restrictions for what was permissible on the Sabbath. Yet, the Pharisees exonerated the priests of any wrongdoing. Even under the Pharisees' own hyper-legalistic standard, some Sabbath violations were allowable and even considered necessary.

The Lord's statement that "something greater than the temple is here" was nothing less than a statement of His deity. The only One greater than the temple (which symbolized the presence of God among His people) was God Himself. As the One greater than the temple, Jesus wielded the divine authority to condemn the practices of the Pharisees.

THE SOVEREIGN INTERPRETER

Jesus said to them, "The Sabbath was made for man, and not man for the Sabbath. So the Son of Man is Lord even of the Sabbath." (vv. 27–28)

God never intended ceremony, ritual, and tradition to stand in the way of mercy, kindness, and goodness toward others. Thus, Jesus explained to the Pharisees that even originally "the Sabbath was made for man, and not man for the Sabbath." God's purpose for the Sabbath day was to give His people a weekly rest. But the Pharisees had turned a divine blessing into a dreaded burden.

Matthew 12:7 notes that Jesus also told the Pharisees, "But if you had known what this means, 'I desire compassion, and not a sacrifice,' you would not have condemned the innocent." Quoting from a portion of Hosea 6:6, Jesus reminded His hearers that God designed the Sabbath to be a merciful day of spiritual reflection and physical recuperation for the people. By turning it into a burdensome day of restrictive observance, the Pharisees obscured its true purpose. The reality was that they were the real violators of the Sabbath. Their indifference to the needs of Jesus' disciples, and their feigned indignation over the fact that their customs had been violated, demonstrated the bankruptcy and ungodliness of their religion.

The conflict was already at a fever pitch when Jesus escalated the matter even higher. In verse 28, He declared to them, "So the Son of Man is Lord even of the Sabbath." Without caveat or apology, Jesus claimed to be the sovereign ruler over the Sabbath. If there had been any ambiguity about His earlier claim, that "something greater than the temple was here" (Matt. 12:6), it was gone. Jesus was clearly claiming to be God, the Creator, and the One who designated the Sabbath in the first place and the sovereign over it (cf. John 1:1–3). He was the Son of Man, a messianic title from Daniel 7:13–14, the divine King who created the Sabbath and defined its parameters. The Pharisees prided themselves on being the authoritative interpreters of God's Word and will. But in their midst stood the One whose interpretation was infinitely more authoritative: the Son of God Himself.

As God in human flesh, He condemned their self-righteous attempts to please God. He was characterized by grace; they prided themselves on their works. He demonstrated mercy and compassion to people; they cared only about protecting their petty customs. He exemplified the true purpose of the Sabbath; they twisted a divine blessing into a dismal day of drudgery.

For the Pharisees, the Sabbath belonged to them. For centuries they had been working out its rules. When Jesus elevated Himself far above them and their rules by declaring Himself to be the Lord of the Sabbath, their hostility and hatred could not be satisfied until they had Him murdered.

———∞———

Chapter 6

CHRIST'S AUTHORITY OVER CREATION

MATTHEW 14:22–33

Immediately He made the disciples get into the boat and go ahead of Him to the other side, while He sent the crowds away. After He had sent the crowds away, He went up on the mountain by Himself to pray; and when it was evening, He was there alone. But the boat was already a long distance from the land, battered by the waves; for the wind was contrary. And in the fourth watch of the night He came to them, walking on the sea. When the disciples saw Him walking on the sea, they were terrified, and said, "It is a ghost!" And they cried out in fear. But immediately Jesus spoke to them, saying, "Take courage, it is I; do not be afraid." Peter said to Him, "Lord, if it is You, command me to come to You on the water." And He said, "Come!" And Peter got out of the boat, and walked on the water and came toward Jesus. But seeing the wind, he became frightened, and beginning to sink, he cried out, "Lord, save me!" Immediately Jesus stretched out His hand and took hold of him, and said to him, "You of little faith, why did you doubt?" When they got into the boat, the wind stopped. And those who were in the boat worshiped Him, saying, "You are certainly God's Son!" (14:22–33)

Many consider the climax of this dramatic event to be Jesus walking on water. Others think it is found in the instant calming of the churning sea. But they are wrong. As important as those elements are, the pinnacle of this passage is the disciples' worship of Jesus as they confess, "You are certainly God's Son" (v. 33).

Though the Father had declared Jesus "My beloved Son" at His baptism (3:17) and even the demons at Gadara had addressed Him as "the Son of God" (8:29), this was the first time the Twelve unequivocally declared their Master to be God's Son.

Within the events of Matthew 14:22–33 are five demonstrations, or proofs, of Jesus' deity that led to the disciples' confession. Within the period of but a few hours they received unmistakable verifications of Jesus' divine authority, divine knowledge, divine protection, divine love, and divine power.

PROOF OF HIS DIVINE AUTHORITY

Immediately He made the disciples get into the boat and go ahead of Him to the other side, while He sent the crowds away. After He had sent the crowds away, He went up on the mountain by Himself to pray; and when it was evening, He was there alone. (14:22–23)

The first affirmation of Jesus' deity on this occasion was His demonstration of divine authority. The fact that Jesus "made the disciples get into the boat" strongly suggests they were reluctant to leave Him and perhaps had argued with Him about it. As soon as the five thousand men, along with the women and children, had been fed and the twelve baskets of leftovers picked up (vv. 19–21), the multitude said, "This is truly the Prophet who is to come into the world" and "they were intending to come and take Him by force to make Him king" (John 6:14–15a). To prevent that from happening, Jesus "withdrew again to the mountain by Himself alone" (v. 15b). He was indeed the predicted King, but He would not establish His earthly kingdom at that time. In any case, it was not the crowd's prerogative to crown Him.

The Crowd and Disciples Yearn for an Earthly King

The disciples no doubt thought the recognition of the crowd was long overdue and rejoiced that Jesus was at last being acknowledged as the Messiah, the coming King who would overthrow the Herods and Rome and establish Israel in her rightful place of world leadership. Jesus Himself had taught them to pray for the kingdom to come (Matt. 6:10), and this seemed an opportune time for Him to begin making the answer to that prayer a reality.

The disciples were also probably thinking of the high positions they would have as Jesus' chief administrators in the kingdom and of the prestige and power those offices would bring. They had suffered indifference and indignities with the Lord for some two years, while living from hand to mouth. Now that the crowd was at fever pitch in support of Jesus, what better time could there be to make His first public move toward the throne? It seems certain that the worldly, self-centered, and ambitious Judas, in particular, would have strongly fostered such thinking among his fellow disciples.

Knowing their thoughts and the growing influence of the crowd on them, Jesus removed them from the evil solicitation by commanding them to "get into the boat and go ahead of Him to the other side." At least in part because of their susceptibility to the political plans of the people, He made the disciples leave.

John identifies the specific destination on the other side as Capernaum (6:24) and Mark as Gennesaret (6:53), a small, fertile plain on the western shore of the Sea of Galilee between Capernaum and Magdala. It was a short trip across the northern tip of the sea, one that most of the disciples had made many times. But they resisted leaving now, not only because of the enthusiasm of the crowd to make Jesus king but also because they did not want to be separated from Jesus. Although they were weak in faith and easily influenced, they nevertheless were deeply devoted to the Lord and felt incomplete and vulnerable when He was not with them. They may also have not wanted to leave then because they could feel the wind starting to blow and were cautious about making even that short trip after dark in bad weather.

Submitting to Jesus' Authority

But regardless of the reasons for their reluctance, the disciples got into the boat and departed. They were under the Lord's authority, but He did not have to use supernatural force to make them leave. His firm word was enough, and it is to their credit that they obeyed. When He told them to cross over ahead of Him to the other side, that is what they did.

Jesus also demonstrated His divine authority over the multitudes, who, despite their great numbers (probably twenty-five thousand or more including the women and children), could not make Jesus do anything contrary to His Father's plan and will. After He sent the disciples on their way to Capernaum, He sent the thousands away as well. They were determined to make Him king in their own way and for their own purposes, but they could not. Without argument or fanfare, He simply dispersed the multitudes, and they bedded down for the night wherever they could near Bethsaida Julias, a few miles inland from the northeast shore of the lake.

Communing with the Father

"After He had sent the crowds away, He went up on the mountain by Himself to pray; and when it was evening, He was there alone." Jesus had little time to rest or to spend unhurried hours with the disciples. He only had time to pray, after which He would miraculously encounter the disciples in the middle of the furious wind at sea.

Jesus' temptations neither began nor ended in the wilderness immediately after His baptism. At the end of that session, the devil only "he left Him until an opportune time" (Luke 4:13). The enthusiasm of the crowds and the disciples to make Him king was very much like the third temptation in the wilderness, in which Satan offered Jesus "all the kingdoms of the world and their glory" (Matt. 4:8–9). "What better time to establish your kingdom than the Passover season, and in what better way than by marching triumphantly into Jerusalem at the head of thousands of faithful, enthusiastic supporters?" the devil may have asked. Jesus would surely gather many more thousands on the way to the Holy City, and His supernatural power would guarantee victory against any opposition. He could easily conquer the Herods, and even mighty Rome would be no match for the Son of God. He could bypass the cross and avoid the agony of having to take the sin of the world upon Himself.

Whatever thoughts Satan may have tried to put into His mind, Jesus turned His back on that evil just as He did on all other. He then came before His heavenly Father to pray, from whom all authority and honor came.

In a sense He did celebrate a victory, but it was over temptation, not Rome; and He turned His attention to His heavenly Father, whom He joined in intimate, refreshing communion. As in the garden, He doubtlessly longed to be restored to the glorious fellowship He had had with His Father before the world even came into existence (John 17:5). But He had other things yet to do.

At the close of His earthly ministry, Jesus told Peter, "Behold, Satan has demanded permission to sift you like wheat; but I have prayed for you, that your faith may not fail" (Luke 22:31–32). Many times before He did it in His high priestly prayer (John 17:6–26), Jesus prayed for His disciples, and it is likely that He prayed for them on this occasion.

By this time it was the second evening of the day, which lasted from six to nine o'clock. The multitudes had been fed during the earlier evening (Matt. 14:15), which was from three to six. And as it became dark, Jesus was there alone in the mountain.

PROOF OF HIS DIVINE KNOWLEDGE

But the boat was already a long distance from the land, battered by the waves; for the wind was contrary. And in the fourth watch of the night He came to them, walking on the sea. (14:24–25)

The second proof of Jesus' deity was His demonstration of divine knowledge. In obedience to His command, the disciples had entered the boat and headed for the other side of the Sea of Galilee. Soon after they left, however, a violent wind erupted, and they were caught "a long distance from the land." John informs us that the "long distance" recorded here amounted to "about three or four miles" (John 6:19).

Because in a normal trip across the northern end of the Sea of Galilee the boat would not have traveled more than a mile or two from shore at any point, the storm had obviously carried it several miles south, out into the middle of the lake. The disciples and their little craft were being "battered by the waves," and "the wind was contrary," pushing them farther and farther away from their destination and closer and closer to disaster. Whether or not the boat had a sail, it would have been useless in the high winds and tossing waves. The only means of movement was rowing, and they were desperately "straining at the oars" (Mark 6:48) for their very lives.

The Desperate Disciples

The disciples were already confused, frustrated, disillusioned, and disappointed that Jesus had sent them away. Though they must have wondered why He sent them to certain death, the Twelve are to be admired for their obedience and perseverance. Although the night was dark, the sea stormy, and the situation apparently hopeless, they were doing their best to do what the Lord commanded. The worst part was that Jesus was not with them. During a similar storm, they had awakened Him and He "rebuked the winds and the sea, and it became perfectly calm" (Matt. 8:26). But now He was miles away. He probably heard the storm and was aware of their plight; but there seemed no way He could get to them. If all the disciples together could not row against the wind and waves, one man could never do it.

Jesus knew of their situation long before it happened, and He did not have to rush away from prayer in order to be on time to help. The storm and the disciples were equally in His hands, and He knew in advance exactly what He would do with both.

The night was divided into four watches, or shifts. The first was from six to nine, the second from nine to twelve, the third from twelve to three, and the fourth from three to six. The fourth watch of the night therefore included the time just before dawn, indicating the disciples had been at sea for at least nine hours, most of the time battling the wind storm.

Jesus waited a long time before He came to them, just as He waited until Lazarus had been dead for several days before He came to Bethany. In both instances, He could have come much sooner than He did and in both instances He could have performed the ensuing miracle without being present, just as He had done in healing the centurion's servant (Matt. 8:13). He could, of course, have prevented the death of Lazarus and the rising of the wind in the first place. But in His infinite wisdom Jesus purposely allowed Mary and Martha and the disciples to reach the extremity of need before He intervened. He knew everything about all of them, and had known it since before they were born. And He knew infinitely better than they did what was best for their welfare and for God's glory.

The disciples should have been rejoicing with David that, "If I make my bed in Sheol, behold, You are there. If I take the wings of the dawn, if I dwell in the remotest part of the sea, even there Your hand will lead Me, and Your right hand will lay hold of me" (Ps. 139:8–10). The Twelve should have remembered that "the LORD also will be a stronghold for the oppressed, a stronghold in times of trouble" (Ps. 9:9), that the Lord was their fortress and deliverer and their rock of refuge (Ps. 18:2), and that He would keep them safe even as they walked "through the valley of the shadow of death" (Ps. 23:4).

But in the turmoil of the night, the Twelve had forgotten those psalms and the Lord's power that they extol. They had little confidence that the Lord, who had known all about the suffering of His people in Egypt and did not forsake them, was relevant in that storm. They saw no relation between their plight and the fact that God had provided a substitute for Isaac when he faced death.

The Caring Jesus

The disciples had even forgotten Jesus' own assurance that their heavenly Father knew all their needs before they asked Him (Matt. 6:32) and that not even a single sparrow "will fall to the ground apart from your Father" and that "the very hairs of your head are all numbered" (10:29–30). All they could think of was their danger, and all they could feel was fear.

But Jesus had not forgotten the disciples, and He came to them through the very danger that threatened to destroy them, walking on the sea. He used the trial as His footpath. He could not physically see them from the mountain or through the stormy darkness, but He knew exactly where they were. God's vision is not like ours, because "the eyes of the LORD are in every place, watching the evil and the good" (Prov. 15:3). "There is no creature hidden from His sight, but all things are open and laid bare to the eyes of Him with whom we have to do" (Heb. 4:13).

PROOF OF HIS DIVINE PROTECTION

When the disciples saw Him walking on the sea, they were terrified, and said, "It is a ghost!" And they cried out in fear. But immediately Jesus spoke to them, saying, "Take courage, it is I; do not be afraid." (14:26–27)

The third proof of Jesus' deity was manifested in His protection of the disciples. As He first approached them, they thought they were getting anything but help, because, "when the disciples saw Him walking on the sea, they were terrified, and said, 'It is a ghost!' And they cried out in fear." The Greek word *theōreō* (from which "saw" is derived) means to look intently, indicating that the disciples' gaze was transfixed on the apparition before them.

Recognizing the Master

At first Jesus did not walk directly toward the boat but appeared to be passing by (Mark 6:48); but that made little difference to the disciples. For a ghost to be anywhere near them was enough to make them frightened almost out of their senses. The term "ghost" is the Greek *phantasma*, which refers to an apparition, a creature of the imagination, and is the word from which come the English *phantom* and *phantasm*.

Many liberal interpreters insist that the disciples only *thought* they saw Jesus walking across the water as their tired and frightened minds played tricks on them. But it would have been quite impossible for all twelve of them to simultaneously experience the same imagined apparition. And such an explanation hardly accounts for the fact that Jesus somehow got into the boat with them, and that as soon as He did the storm instantly ceased. The writers make a point of the fact that the boat was a great distance from the shore. Neither, as some suggest, could the disciples have seen Jesus walking along the beach while appearing to be walking on the water— even in broad daylight. Either they lied in reporting the event or it occurred as they said it did.

Because of the darkness, the mist from the wind and waves, the fatigue from rowing, and the fear that already gripped them because of the storm, they did not recognize Jesus when He appeared to them. Mark reports that "they all saw Him" (Mark 6:50), but none of them suspected it was Jesus. And their fear of drowning now turned into abject terror as they beheld the form they thought was a ghost come to add to their torment. In the dark before the dawn, hopelessness turned to utter horror and despair. In their panic they could not help but cry out for fear.

Although Jesus was testing the disciples' faith, He understood their frailty. He calmed their fear by saying simply, "Take courage, it is I; do not be afraid." In spite of the raging winds, the waves battering against the boat, and their fear-stricken minds, they immediately recognized their Master's voice.

It was not the time for an explanation of why He was there, of what He planned to do next, or of why He had not come sooner. It was time to give courage, to still the storm that raged within the disciples, even before stilling the one that raged around them.

Trusting the Sovereign Savior

Jesus did not have to walk on the water to save them, but His doing so gave them an unforgettable reminder of the power and extent of His divine protection. He did not approach the boat in a raging windstorm to teach them to walk on water but to teach them that God can and will act on behalf of His own.

We will never find ourselves in a place where Christ cannot find us; and no storm is too severe for Him to save us from it. He protects His own, whom He will never fail or forsake (Josh. 1:5; Heb. 13:5). The lesson for the disciples is the lesson for us: There is no reason for God's people to fear. There is no reason for anxiety, no matter how hopeless and threatening our problems seem to be. Life is often stormy and painful, often threatening and frightening. Some believers suffer more than others, but all suffer at some time and in some way. In spite of that, the storm is never so severe, the night never so black, and the boat never so frail that we risk danger beyond our Father's care.

When the apostle Paul was on the ship taking him to Rome to appear before Caesar, it encountered an exceptionally violent storm in the Mediterranean Sea near the island of Crete. After the crew had thrown all the cargo, tackle, supplies, and food overboard, the ship was still in danger of foundering on the rocks. Paul had warned they should remain in the safety of the port at Fair Havens through the winter, but his advice was not heeded by the centurion or the pilot of the ship. When everyone else on board had despaired of reaching land alive, an angel appeared to Paul assuring him that, although the ship would be lost, no lives would be. Yet even before the angel's message, Paul, unlike the fearful disciples, was at perfect peace and offered encouragement to those on the ship with him, saying, "Keep up your courage, men, for I believe God that it will turn out exactly as I have been told" (Acts 27:25).

Similarly, the disciples who were reluctant to leave Jesus and go to Capernaum obeyed by rowing out into the storm they knew was coming, and Jesus honored their faithfulness. When believers are in the place of obedience they are in the place of safety, no matter what the circumstances. The place of security is not the place of favorable circumstance but the place of obedience to God's will. Yet their courage and faith, when put to the test of the wild winds and waves, failed them and the Master had to reassure them of His presence. And He did.

PROOF OF HIS DIVINE LOVE

Peter said to Him, "Lord, if it is You, command me to come to You on the water." And He said, "Come!" And Peter got out of the boat, and walked on the water and came toward Jesus. But seeing the wind, he became frightened, and beginning to sink, he cried out, "Lord, save me!" Immediately Jesus stretched out His hand and took hold of him, and said to him, "You of little faith, why did you doubt?" (14:28–31)

The fourth proof of Jesus' deity was His demonstration of divine love. Although Mark and John report Jesus' walking on the water, only Matthew tells of this incident concerning Peter.

Peter's Motive

Peter's "if" did not reflect doubt that it was actually his Lord, because going out onto the water to join an unidentified ghost was the last thing Peter would have done. He was naturally impetuous and brash, and more than once his overconfidence got him into trouble, including trouble with the Lord. But it would have taken more than brashness for this lifelong fisherman to have ventured out on the water without benefit or a boat, because no one on board better knew the dangers of Galilee storms than Peter. He had probably been thrown into the water at times by high winds or waves and had seen others experience the same trauma. He was no fool, and it is highly unlikely that his impulsiveness would have so easily overridden his reason and instinctive caution.

His Joy

It seems much more probable that Peter was overjoyed to see Jesus and that his supreme concern was to be safely with Him. Mere impetuosity might have caused him to jump out of the boat, expecting Jesus somehow to come to his rescue. But he knew better, and he therefore asked the Lord, "Command me to come to You on the water." He knew Jesus had the power to enable him to walk on the water, but he did not presume to attempt the feat without His express instruction. Peter's request was an act of affection built on confident faith. He did not ask to walk on water for the sake of doing something spectacular, but because it was the way to get to Jesus.

His Love, Courage, and Faith

Peter did many things for which he can be faulted. But he is sometimes faulted for things that reflect love, courage, and faith as much as brashness or cowardice. For instance, although he denied the Lord while in the courtyard during Jesus' trial, he was nevertheless there, as close to Him as he could get. The rest of the disciples were nowhere to be found. On the Mount of Transfiguration, Peter's suggestion was unwise but it was prompted by sincere devotion: "Lord, it is good for us to be here; if You wish, I will make three tabernacles here, one for You, and one for Moses, and one for Elijah" (Matt. 17:4). He genuinely loved Jesus and sincerely wanted to serve and please Him. Peter did not resist Jesus' washing his feet because of pride, but because, in his deep humility, he could not conceive of his Lord washing the feet of anyone so unworthy. And when Jesus explained the significance of what He was doing, Peter said, "Lord, then wash not only my feet, but also my hands and my head" (John 13:9).

Peter was continually in the Lord's shadow and footsteps. By reading between the lines of the gospel accounts it is not difficult to imagine that Peter sometimes followed so closely behind Jesus that he bumped into Him when He stopped. Peter sensed in Jesus' presence a wonderful safety and comfort, and that is where Peter now wanted to be. It was safer to be with Jesus on the water than to be without Him in the boat.

His Imperfect but Real Love

Peter's love for Jesus was imperfect and weak, but it was real. It was his primary motive in all he did. Three times Jesus asked Peter if he loved Him, and each time Peter responded affirmatively. Jesus did not contradict Peter's answer but reminded him of his obligation to care for his Master's sheep and warned him of the great cost his love would demand (John 21:15–18). Tradition has it that when Peter was about to be crucified, he requested being put on the cross upside down, not feeling worthy to die in the same way as his Lord.

Jesus' telling Peter to "come" confirms the disciple's right motive. Jesus never invites, much less commands, a person to do anything sinful. Nor is He ever a party to pride or presumption. With the greatest of compassion, Jesus told Peter to come, highly pleased that he wanted to be with his Lord.

As much as anything else, it was Peter's great love for Christ that made him the leader of the disciples. He appears to have been the closest to Christ, and is always named first in lists of the Twelve. Just as the Lord never rejects weak faith, but accepts it and builds on it, He also never rejects weak and imperfect love. With great patience and care He takes the love of His children and, through trials and hardships as well as successes and victories, builds that love into greater conformity to His own love.

Jesus' telling Peter, "Come!" was an act of love. John declared, "We have come to know and have believed the love which God has for us." In fact, he goes on to say, "God is love" (1 John 4:16; cf. v. 8). It is God's nature to be loving, just as it is water's nature to be wet and the sun's to be bright and hot. He loves His own with an infinite, uninfluenced, unqualified, unchanging, unending, and perfect love.

Christians most perfectly reflect their heavenly Father when they are loving, especially to each other. "If someone says, 'I love God,' and hates his brother, he is a liar," John continues to explain; "for the one who does not love his brother whom he has seen, cannot love God whom he has not seen" (1 John 4:20).

Peter's Faith Tested

Although Peter was sincere, he did not comprehend the reality or the extremity of what he was asking to do. From the relative safety of the boat the feat did not seem so terrifying; but once "Peter got out of the boat, and walked on the water and came toward Jesus," the situation appeared radically different. Peter temporarily took his eyes off the Lord and, "seeing the wind, he became frightened, and beginning to sink, he cried out, saying, 'Lord, save me!'" His faith was enough to get him out of the boat, but it was not enough to carry him across the water.

Faith is strengthened by its being taken to extremities it has never faced before. Such strengthening is basic to Christian growth and maturity. "Blessed is a man who perseveres under trial," James says, "for once he has been approved, he will receive the crown of life which the Lord has promised to those who love Him" (James 1:12). The Lord takes us as far as our faith will go, and when it ends we begin to sink. It is then that we call out to Him and He again demonstrates His faithfulness and His power, and our faith learns to extend that much further. As we trust God in the faith we have, we discover its limitations; but we also discover what it can yet become.

When Peter began to sink, he was probably fully clothed and would have had great difficulty swimming through the high waves. And in his fright he could think of nothing but drowning. But as soon as he cried out, "Lord, save me," he was safe, because "immediately Jesus stretched out His hand and took hold of him."

When Jesus rebuked him, saying, "You of little faith, why did you doubt?" Peter must have wondered at the question. The reason for his doubt seemed obvious. He was bone weary from rowing most of the night, scared to death by the storm and then by what he thought was a ghost, and now it seemed he was about to drown before he could reach the Lord. He had never been in such a situation before, and it may be that his actually walking a few feet on the water added to his shock.

But Peter's weak faith was better than no faith; and, as in the courtyard when he denied the Lord, at least he was there and not holding back like the rest. He at least started toward Jesus, and when he faltered, the Lord took him the rest of the way.

Jesus had been interceding for Peter and the others while He was on the mountain, and now He came directly to their aid in the midst of the storm. The Lord goes before us and He goes with us. When we get frustrated, anxious, bewildered, and frightened, Satan tempts us to wonder why God allows such things to happen to His children. And if we keep our attention on those things we will begin to sink just as surely as Peter did. But if we cry out to the Lord for help, He will come to our rescue just as surely as He did to Peter's.

Peter would one day write, "In this you greatly rejoice, even though now for a little while, if necessary, you have been distressed by various trials, so that the proof of your faith, being more precious than gold which is perishable, even though tested by fire, may be found to result in praise and glory and honor at the revelation of Jesus Christ" (1 Peter 1:6–7).

PROOF OF HIS DIVINE POWER

When they got into the boat, the wind stopped. And those who were in the boat worshiped Him, saying, "You are certainly God's Son!" (14:32–33)

The most spectacular miracle was accomplished without Jesus saying a word or raising a hand. The moment He and Peter got into the boat with the other disciples, the wind stopped. It was as if the wind was simply waiting for the miracle to be finished; and when it had served its purpose, it stopped.

Just as instantaneously, "the boat was at the land to which they were going" (John 6:21). They had been three or four miles out to sea and the storm was still raging as fiercely as ever; but in an instant it stopped and the boat was at its destination. On the basis of normal human experience it is hardly surprising that the disciples "were utterly astonished" (Mark 6:51). But the disciples had been having astounding displays of Jesus' miraculous power for two years, and for them these remarkable events should not have been astonishing. We learn from Mark that their amazement resulted from their not having "gained any insight from the incident of the loaves"—or from Jesus' earlier stilling of the storm or from any other great work He had done—because "their heart was hardened" (Mark 6:52).

Yet in that moment those same hearts were softened and those eyes opened as they had never been before; "and those who were in the boat worshiped Him, saying, 'You are certainly God's Son!'" They were now more than simply amazed, as the crowds and they themselves had always been. They were taken past amazement to worship, which is what Jesus' signs and miracles were intended to produce. At last they were beginning to see Jesus as the One whom God highly exalted and on whom He "bestowed . . . the name which is above every name." As the apostle Paul would later declare, one day upon hearing the name of Jesus "every knee will bow, of those who are in heaven and on earth and under the earth, and . . . every tongue will confess that Jesus Christ is Lord, to the glory of God the Father" (Phil. 2:9–11).

PART 3

———✦———

THE DIVINE
CLAIMS OF CHRIST

———∞———

Chapter 7

SON OF MAN AND SON OF GOD

MATTHEW 16:13–17

Now when Jesus came into the district of Caesarea Philippi, He was asking His disciples, "Who do people say that the Son of Man is?" And they said, "Some say John the Baptist; and others, Elijah; but still others, Jeremiah, or one of the prophets." He said to them, "But who do you say that I am?" Simon Peter answered, "You are the Christ, the Son of the living God." And Jesus said to him, "Blessed are you, Simon Barjona, because flesh and blood did not reveal this to you, but My Father who is in heaven. (16:13–17)

This passage represents the climax of Jesus' teaching ministry. It is, in effect, the apostles' final examination, consisting of but one question, the ultimate question that every human being must face: Who is Jesus Christ? A person's answer is of the most monumental importance, because on it hinges his eternal destiny. It is a question that no one can escape or avoid. Every soul, as it were, will be pinned against the wall of eternity and forced to answer that question.

For some two and a half years Jesus had been moving to this moment—teaching and reteaching, affirming and reaffirming, demonstrating and re-demonstrating, building and rebuilding the truth of who He was in order to establish it completely and securely in the minds and hearts of the Twelve.

During the previous several months the Lord had largely shunned the crowds and the Jewish leaders. His few encounters with them were brief and terse. The misguided multitudes wanted to make Him their political deliverer from the military bondage of Rome and the capricious ambitions of Herod. The scribes, Pharisees, and Sadducees were, for the most part, thoroughly convinced He was a threat to their religious system and were determined to be rid of Him, if necessary by taking His life.

As He spent more and more time alone with the Twelve, Jesus went more often into Gentile territory and stayed longer. He withdrew to the fringes of Palestine in order to be free of the misguided and fickle adulation of the multitudes and the growing hostility of the Jewish religious leaders.

THE SETTING

Now when Jesus came into the district of Caesarea Philippi, (16:13a)

The city of Caesarea Philippi was originally named Paneas (or Panias), after the Greek god Pan, who, according to pagan mythology, was born in a nearby cave. Caesar Augustus had given the region to Herod the Great, who built a temple in Paneas in honor of the emperor. Herod's son, Philip the tetrarch, inherited the land, greatly enlarged the city, and renamed it after Caesar. He added the name Philippi both to gain honor for himself and to distinguish this Caesarea from the one on the Mediterranean coast west of Jerusalem.

Caesarea Philippi was located about twenty-five miles northeast of the Sea of Galilee and forty miles southwest of Damascus, on a beautiful plateau near the headwaters of the Jordan River. A few miles to the north, snow-covered Mount Hermon rose to a height of more than 9,000 feet above sea level. On clear days the majestic mountain can easily be seen from northern Galilee towns such as Capernaum, Cana, and Nazareth.

Caesarea Philippi was but a few miles from the ancient Jewish city of Dan, which for centuries had been considered the northernmost boundary of the Promised Land, the southernmost being Beersheba (see Judg. 20:1; 1 Chron. 21:2). On the north it was the last outpost of Israel and had always been especially susceptible to pagan influence.

The location provided Jesus and the disciples welcome relief from the hot Galilean lowlands and from the pressure of the Jewish leaders and the threat from Herod Antipas.

From Luke 9:18 we learn that Jesus posed His all-important question to the disciples just after He had spent time praying alone, and from Mark 8:27 that the group had not yet arrived in the city of Caesarea Philippi proper but were passing through some of the villages on the outskirts. At this crossroads of heathenism and Judaism Jesus left a time of intimate fellowship with His heavenly Father and confronted His disciples with the question that every person and every religion must one day answer.

THE EXAMINATION

He was asking His disciples, "Who do people say that the Son of Man is?" And they said, "Some say John the Baptist; and others,

**Elijah; but still others, Jeremiah, or one of the prophets." He
said to them, "But who do you say that I am?"** (16:13b–15)

"Son of Man" was Jesus' most common designation of Himself
and is used of Him some eighty times in the New Testament. It was
clearly recognized by Jews as a title of the Messiah (see Dan. 7:13);
but because it emphasized His humanness, many Jews preferred
not to use it. No doubt it was for that reason that Jesus *did* prefer
it—to focus on the humiliation and submission of His first coming
and His work of sacrificial, substitutionary atonement.

Jesus' priority ministry in the world was to reveal Himself, to
teach and to demonstrate who He was. He therefore began the ex-
amination by asking His disciples, "Who do people say that the
Son of Man is?" The people to whom the Lord referred were the
Jews, God's chosen people, to whom the Messiah was sent first
(Rom. 1:16; cf. John 4:22).

It was not that Jesus was unaware of what the people were saying about Him but that He wanted the Twelve to think carefully
about those popular perceptions. He was not concerned about the
opinions of the unbelieving and hypocritical scribes and Pharisees,
some of whom had even accused Him of being in league with Satan
(Matt. 10:25; 12:24). He was rather asking about the thoughts of
those who looked on Him positively, although uncertainly, and
who recognized Him to be more than an ordinary religious leader.
After hearing His teaching and witnessing His miracles, what was
their final verdict about Jesus, the Son of Man?

"Some say John the Baptist," the Twelve replied. Perhaps following the frightened assessment of Herod the tetrarch (Matt.
14:1–2), some of the Jews believed Jesus was a reincarnated John
the Baptist, come back from the grave to continue his ministry of

announcing the Messiah. Like Herod, those people recognized that Jesus' miraculous power was unexplainable on a human basis.

Others believed Jesus was a reincarnated Elijah, considered by most Jews to be the supreme Old Testament prophet, whom the Lord was to send again "before the coming of the great and terrible day of the LORD" (Mal. 4:5). In modern Jewish Passover celebrations an empty chair is reserved at the table for Elijah, in the hope of his one day coming to announce the Messiah's arrival.

Still others said Jesus was Jeremiah, another of the most revered prophets. In the apocryphal book of 2 Maccabees (2:4–8), Jeremiah is said to have taken the ark of the covenant and the altar of incense out of the Temple and hidden them on Mount Nebo in order to preserve them from desecration and destruction by the Babylonians. Some Jews thought that before the Messiah returned to establish His kingdom, Jeremiah would return to earth and restore the ark and the altar to their proper places in the Temple. The same apocryphal book pictures a white-bearded Jeremiah handing a golden sword to the great Jewish hero Judas Maccabaeus to use in overthrowing the Greeks (15:12–16).

Some of the people perhaps saw in Jesus something of the character and message of John the Baptist. Some saw in Him the fire and intensity of Elijah; and still others saw in Him the lament and grief of Jeremiah. In all three of those identities, however, Jesus was thought to be only the Messiah's forerunner, who had come back to life with God-given miraculous powers.

The rest of the people who recognized Jesus' uniqueness did not speculate about His particular identity but simply considered Him to be one of the prophets who was "risen again" (see Luke 9:19).

In each instance the people considered Jesus to be a forerunner of the Messiah but not the Messiah Himself. They could not deny His supernatural power, but they would not accept Him as Messiah and Savior. They came as close to God's ultimate truth as they could without fully recognizing and accepting it.

Since Jesus' day, much of the world has similarly wanted to speak highly of Him without recognizing His deity and lordship. Pilate said, "I find no guilt in this man" (Luke 23:4). Napoleon said, "I know men, and Jesus was no mere man." Diderot referred to Jesus as "the unsurpassed," Strauss, the German rationalist, as "the highest model of religion," John Stuart Mill as "the guide of humanity," the French atheist Renan as "the greatest among the sons of men," Theodore Parker as "a youth with God in His heart," and Robert Owens as "the irreproachable one." Some in our own day have called Him the ultimate Superstar. But all those titles and descriptions fall short of identifying Jesus as He fully is—the Messiah, God in human flesh.

After the disciples reported what the multitudes were saying about Him, Jesus then asked, "But who do you say that I am?" The Twelve knew that most of the people's views of Jesus were inadequate. Now they had to answer for themselves.

THE CONFESSION

Simon Peter answered, "You are the Christ, the Son of the living God." (16:16)

As usual (see, e.g., Matt. 15:15; 19:27; John 6:68), Simon Peter was the spokesman, "the director of the apostolic choir," as Chrysostom called him. Also as usual, his comments were brief, emphatic, and decisive: "You are the Christ, the Son of the living God." *Christ* is the Greek equivalent of the Hebrew *Messiah*, God's predicted and long-awaited deliverer of Israel, the supreme "Anointed One," the coming High Priest, King, Prophet, and Savior. Without hesitation Peter declared Jesus to be the Messiah, whereas the multitudes of Jews believed Him to be only the Messiah's precursor.

On first meeting Jesus, Andrew had excitedly proclaimed Him to be the Messiah, and Nathaniel had called Him "the Son of God … the King of Israel" (John 1:41, 49). The disciples knew that John the Baptist had testified that Jesus "is the Son of God" (John 1:34), and the longer they stayed with Him, the more evidence they had of His divine nature, power, and authority.

Like their fellow Jews, however, they had been taught to expect a conquering and reigning Messiah who would deliver God's people from their enemies and establish forever His righteous kingdom on earth. And when Jesus refused to use His miraculous power for His own benefit or to oppose the Roman oppressors, the disciples wondered if they were right about Jesus' identity. His humility, meekness, and subservience were in total contrast to their preconceived views of the Messiah. That the Messiah would be ridiculed with impunity, not to mention persecuted and executed, was inconceivable. When Jesus spoke of His going away and coming back, Thomas doubtlessly echoed the consternation of all the disciples when he said, "Lord, we do not know where You are going, how do we know the way?" (John 14:5).

It was similar bewilderment that caused John the Baptist to question his earlier affirmation of Jesus' messiahship. "When John, while imprisoned, heard of the works of Christ, he sent word by his disciples and said to Him, 'Are You the Expected One, or shall we look for someone else?'" (Matt. 11:2–3). Jesus' miracles were clear evidence of His messiahship, but His failure to use those powers to overthrow Rome and establish His earthly kingdom brought Jesus' identity into question even with the godly, Spirit-filled John.

Like John the Baptist, the Twelve fluctuated between moments of great faith and of grave doubt. They could proclaim with deep conviction, "Lord, to whom shall we go? You have words of eternal life. We have believed and have come to know that You are the Holy One of God" (John 6:68–69). They could also display remarkable lack of faith and discernment, even after witnessing hundreds of healings and dramatic demonstrations of supernatural power (see Matt. 8:26; 14:31; 16:8). They were sometimes strong in faith and sometimes weak. Jesus frequently spoke of their "little faith."

Now, at last, the truth of Jesus' divinity and messiahship was established in their minds beyond question. They would still experience times of weakness and confusion about what Jesus said and did, but they would no longer doubt who it was who said and did them. He was indeed the Christ, the Son of the living God. God's own Spirit had now imbedded the truth indelibly in their hearts.

It took two and a half years for them to come to this place of confession, through the struggles and hatred of the Jewish religious leaders, the mounting fickleness and rejection of the people, and their own confusion about what the Messiah had come to do. But without question they now knew He was the fulfiller of their hopes, the source of their salvation, the desire of the nations.

On behalf of all the apostles, Peter not only confessed Jesus as the Messiah, the Christ, but also as the Son of the living God. The Son of Man (v. 13) was also the Son of God, the Creator of the universe and all that is in it. He was the true and real God, not a mythological figment such as Pan or a mortal "deity" such as Caesar—both of whom had shrines in Caesarea Philippi. The disciples' Lord was Son of the living God.

As evidenced by numerous things the Twelve later said and

did, they did not at this time have a full comprehension of the Trinity or even of the full nature and work of Christ. But they knew Jesus was truly the Christ and that He was truly divine, the Son of the living God. Son reflects the idea of oneness in essence, because a son is one in nature with his father. So Jesus Christ was one in nature with God the Father (cf. John 5:17–18; 10:30–33).

THE RESULT

And Jesus said to him, "Blessed are you, Simon Barjona," (16:17a)

Those who truly confess that Jesus is God, which is to confess Him as Lord and Savior (1 John 4:14–15), are divinely and eternally blessed. They are "blessed . . . with every spiritual blessing in the heavenly places in Christ," chosen "in Him before the foundation of the world . . . [to] be holy and blameless before Him," and "in love [are] predestined . . . to adoption as sons through Jesus Christ to Himself" (Eph. 1:3–5). God pours out all His supernatural resources on those who come to Him through faith in His Son, because through Him they become God's own children.

Emphasizing Peter's human inadequacy, Jesus called him by his original family name, Simon Barjona, the second part of the name being an Aramaic term that meant son of Jonah (or John).

THE SOURCE

"because flesh and blood did not reveal this to you, but My Father who is in heaven." (16:17b)

The disciples were not finally convinced of Jesus' messiahship and divinity because of His teaching or His miracles, amazing as those were. Those things alone were not sufficient to convince the Twelve, just as they were not sufficient to convince the thousands of other people who heard the same truth and witnessed the same miracles but failed to accept and follow the one who taught and performed them. Man's human capabilities, here represented by the metonym "flesh and blood," cannot bring understanding of the things of God (cf. 1 Cor. 2:14). The Father Himself must reveal them and bring understanding of His Son to human minds.

From the gospel accounts it seems clear that the Father disclosed the Son primarily through the Son Himself. There is no record or intimation that any divine revelation was given to the Twelve during Jesus' earthly ministry other than that given through Jesus Himself. As the light of Jesus' teaching and the significance of His miraculous power began to dawn on them, the Spirit opened their minds to see Him as the Messiah, the Son of the living God.

Jesus had made many astounding claims about Himself. He declared that He Himself had come to fulfill the law and the prophets (Matt. 5:17) and that in the last days many people will address Him as Lord (7:22). He said, "I am the living bread that came down out of heaven; if anyone eats of this bread, he will live forever" (John 6:51), and, "I am the door; if anyone enters through Me, he will be saved" (10:9; cf. 14:6).

Jesus had also performed astounding miracles. He had turned ordinary water into the highest quality wine (John 2:6–11), healed multiple hundreds of every sort of disease (see, e.g., Matt. 4:24; 8:16; 9:35), and even quieted a raging storm with a word (Matt. 8:26).

Perhaps the greatest testimony to Jesus' messiahship, however, was His claim to be Lord of the Sabbath (Matt. 12:8), a claim that for a Jew of His day could only have been interpreted as presumption of deity. The Sabbath, which has the basic meaning of rest or cessation, was the center of Jewish life. Not only their week but also their entire calendar of feasts and holy days was built on the concept of sabbath. The seventh day of the week (Ex. 20:11) and every other sabbath observance was a time of rest and worship. The book of Leviticus mentions nine sabbath-based festivals, which included the weekly Sabbath (Lev. 23:3); the Passover (vv. 4–8); the Feast of Firstfruits (vv. 9–14); Pentecost (vv. 15–22); the Feast of trumpets (vv. 23–25); the Day of Atonement, Yom Kippur (vv. 26–32); the Feast of Tabernacles (vv. 33–44); the sabbatical year (25:2–7); and the Year of Jubilee (vv. 8–55), when, every fiftieth year, all slaves were freed and all land restored to its original owners.

All of those sabbath observances were pictures of the final and eternal rest of the children of God, the time when Messiah would come to earth to set His people free and establish His divine kingdom. Every time a Jew celebrated a sabbath he was reminded that someday he and all his fellow Jews would be released from all bondage, whether the bondage of political oppression, the bondage of continual sacrifices, or the bondage of labor to make a living. The entire sabbath system pointed to the true, perfect, and eternal rest that Messiah would bring to His people.

For Jesus to claim that He fulfilled the prophecy of Isaiah 61:1–2, as He did in the synagogue in Nazareth (Luke 4:18–21), was unmistakably to claim messiahship. For Him to present Himself as the source of rest (Matt. 11:28) was to present Himself as the source of holiness, and to claim lordship over the Sabbath (Matt. 12:8) was to claim lordship over everything.

Because Jesus is Himself God's perfect sabbath rest and the source of true holiness, believers have no more reason to observe the seventh day of the week or any other special day. "For we who have believed enter that rest. . . . So there remains a Sabbath rest for the people of God. For the one who has entered His rest has himself also rested from his works, as God did from His" (Heb. 4:3, 9–10). "Therefore no one is to act as your judge in regard to food or drink or in respect to a festival or a new moon or a Sabbath day," Paul wrote. Such things "are a mere shadow of what is to come; but the substance belongs to Christ" (Col. 2:16–17).

The command to keep the Sabbath day is the only one of the Ten Commandments that the New Testament does not require of Christians. By His grace, Jesus Christ gives every believer in Him a jubilee liberation that is perfect, final, and eternal. A Christian therefore does not violate the Sabbath when he works on the Lord's Day but when he persists in self-righteous works in the presumptuous hope of adding to what the Savior has already accomplished.

"All things have been handed over to Me by My Father," Jesus had explained on an earlier occasion; "and no one knows the Son except the Father; nor does anyone know the Father except the Son, and anyone to whom the Son wills to reveal Him" (Matt. 11:27).

As with the disciples, when people today confess Jesus Christ as Lord and Savior and fellowship with Him through His Word, the Spirit opens their minds and hearts to more and more of His truth and power. "Faith comes from hearing, and hearing by the word of Christ," Paul declared (Rom. 10:17). As we continue to gaze into His glory we are transformed into His image (see Rom. 8:29; 1 Cor. 15:49; Col. 3:10).

Chapter 8

———⚬⚬⚬———

EQUAL WITH GOD

JOHN 5:17–24

But He answered them, "My Father is working until now, and I Myself am working." For this reason therefore the Jews were seeking all the more to kill Him, because He not only was breaking the Sabbath, but also was calling God His own Father, making Himself equal with God. Therefore Jesus answered and was saying to them, "Truly, truly, I say to you, the Son can do nothing of Himself, unless it is something He sees the Father doing; for whatever the Father does, these things the Son also does in like manner. For the Father loves the Son, and shows Him all things that He Himself is doing; and the Father will show Him greater works than these, so that you will marvel. For just as the Father raises the dead and gives them life, even so the Son also gives life to whom He wishes. For not even the Father judges anyone, but He has given all judgment to the Son, so that all will honor the Son even as they honor the Father. He who does not honor the Son does not honor the Father who sent Him. Truly, truly, I say to you, he who hears My word, and believes Him who sent Me, has eternal life, and does not come into judgment, but has passed out of death into life." (5:17–24)

Throughout the centuries, scholars and skeptics have given many different answers to the query, "Who is Jesus Christ?" His life is the most influential ever lived, and its impact continues to escalate. Still, Jesus' true identity is hotly debated by modern historians and theologians. Countless opinions have appeared as unbelievers have attempted to explain away the truth about Him.

THE IDENTITY OF JESUS

The Jewish leaders of Jesus' day, motivated by their own bitter jealousy, accused Him of being a Samaritan who was demon-possessed (John 8:48; cf. 7:20; 8:52), insane (John 10:20), and of illegitimate birth (John 8:41). Although they could not deny Jesus' astonishing power, they discounted it as being of satanic origin (Matt. 12:24). Their successors similarly reviled Jesus as "a transgressor in Israel, who [practiced] magic, scorned the words of the wise, [and] led the people astray."[1]

The Conclusions of Theological Liberals and Existentialists

The theological liberals and skeptics of the eighteenth and nineteenth centuries were intent on denying Jesus' deity. They viewed Him as the quintessential strictly human moral teacher, in whom the spark of divinity inherent in all people burned most brightly. In their minds, Jesus' sacrificial life provided mankind with a model that all should follow, but not with a means by which men might be saved. Thus, He was "an example for faith, not the object of faith."[2]

To twentieth-century existentialists, such as the highly influential Rudolf Bultmann, the Jesus of history was all but unknowable. That did not bother Bultmann, however, since he believed that the "Christ of faith" invented by the church could still provide the basis for a genuine religious experience. Neoorthodox theologians, such as Karl Barth, were not willing to so completely ignore the factual significance of Jesus' life or His deity. Yet they were not willing to accept and believe the biblical record of Christ in a truly historical sense.

Other conceptions of Jesus range from the crusading sociopolitical revolutionary of liberation theology, to the cynical Jewish sage of the Jesus Seminar and the countercultural hero of the rock musicals *Godspell* and *Jesus Christ Superstar*. But all such fanciful and blasphemous viewpoints are far removed from the God-man revealed in holy Scripture. They say more about the imaginations of the people who created them than about Jesus' true identity.

Jesus' Own Testimony

Ironically, in all the debate over Him, Jesus' own testimony is seldom considered reasonably. Did He, as historic Christianity has always maintained, claim to be God incarnate in human flesh? Or, as skeptics argue, did His followers later invent those claims and attribute them to Him? All this unbelieving pseudo scholarship ignores the biblical account of His life and ministry, which leaves no legitimate doubt about who Jesus declared Himself to be, and who He was.

Jesus frequently spoke of His unique, otherworldly origin, of having preexisted in heaven before coming into this world. To the hostile Jews He declared, "You are from below, I am from above; you are of this world, I am not of this world" (John 8:23). "What then," He asked, "if you see the Son of Man ascending to where He was before?" (John 6:62). In His High Priestly Prayer (John 17) Jesus spoke of the glory which He had with the Father before the world existed (v. 5). In John 16:28 He told His disciples, "I came forth from the Father and have come into the world; I am leaving the world again and going to the Father."

Jesus claimed He had the prerogatives of deity. He declared He had control over people's eternal destinies (John 8:24; cf. Luke 12:8–9; John 5:22, 27–29), authority over the divinely-ordained institution of the Sabbath (Matt. 12:8; Mark 2:28; Luke 6:5), and the power to answer prayer (John 14:13–14; cf. Acts 7:59; 9:10–17) Furthermore, Jesus claimed the right to receive worship, faith, and obedience, even as He acknowledged such rights belong to God alone (Matt. 21:16; John 14:1; cf. John 5:23). He also assumed the right to forgive sins (Mark 2:5–11)—something which, as His shocked opponents correctly understood, only God can do (v. 7).

Jesus also called God's angels (Gen. 28:12; Luke 12:8–9; 15:10; John 1:51) His angels (Matt. 13:41; 24:30–31). He called God's elect (Luke 18:7; Rom. 8:33) His elect (Matt. 24:30–31); and He identified God's kingdom as His Kingdom.[3]

When a Samaritan woman said to Him, "I know that Messiah is coming (He who is called Christ); when that One comes, He will declare all things to us" Jesus replied, "I who speak to you am He" (John 4:25–26). In His High Priestly Prayer to the Father, He referred to Himself as "Jesus Christ whom You have sent" (John 17:3); "Christ" is the Greek equivalent of the Hebrew word translated "Messiah." When asked at His trial by the high priest, "Are You the Christ, the Son of the Blessed One?" (Mark 14:61) Jesus replied simply, "I am" (v. 62).

He also accepted, without correction or amendment, the testimonies of Peter (Matt. 16:16–17), Martha (John 11:27), and others (e.g., Matt. 9:27; 20:30–31) that He was the Messiah.

Calling Himself "Son of Man" and "Son of God"

The Lord's favorite description of Himself was "Son of Man" (cf. Matt. 8:20; Mark 2:28; Luke 6:22; John 9:35–37, etc.). Although that title seems to stress His humanity, it also speaks of His deity. Jesus' use of the term derives from Daniel 7:13–14, where the Son of Man is on equal terms with God the Father, the Ancient of Days.

The Jews viewed themselves collectively as sons of God by creation. Jesus, however, claimed to be God's Son by nature. "All things have been handed over to Me by My Father," Jesus affirmed, "and no one knows the Son except the Father; nor does anyone know the Father except the Son, and anyone to whom the Son wills to reveal Him" (Matt. 11:27). In John 5:25–26, He said, "Truly, truly, I say to you, an hour is coming and now is, when the dead will hear the voice of the Son of God, and those who hear will live. For just as the Father has life in Himself, even so He gave to the Son also to have life in Himself." After receiving word that Lazarus was ill Jesus said to the disciples, "This sickness is not to end in death, but for the glory of God, so that the Son of God may be glorified by it" (John 11:4).

When asked at His trial, "Are You the Son of God, then?" Jesus replied, "Yes, I am" (Luke 22:70; cf. Mark 14:61–62). Instead of rejecting the title, the Lord embraced it without apology or embarrassment (Matt. 4:3, 6; 8:29; Mark 3:11–12; Luke 4:41; John 1:49–50; 11:27).

The hostile Jewish authorities clearly understood that Jesus' use of the title Son of God was a claim to deity. Otherwise, they would not have accused Him of blasphemy (cf. John 10:36). In fact, it was Jesus' claim to be the Son of God that led the Jews to demand His death: "The Jews answered [Pilate], 'We have a law, and by that law

He ought to die because He made Himself out to be the Son of God'" (John 19:7). Even while He was on the cross, some mocked Him, sneering, "He trusts in God; let God rescue Him now, if He delights in Him; for He said, 'I am the Son of God'" (Matt. 27:43).

Jesus further outraged the unbelieving Jews by taking for Himself the covenant name of God, "I am" or Yahweh. (For more on the meaning of "I am" and its usage in John's Gospel, see chapter 10.) That name was so sacred to the Jews that they refused even to pronounce it, lest they take it in vain (cf. Ex. 20:7). In John 8:24 Jesus warned that those who refuse to believe He is Yahweh will perish eternally: "Therefore I said to you that you will die in your sins; for unless you believe that I am He, you will die in your sins." (The word "He" is not in the original Greek.) Later in that chapter "Jesus said to [His hearers], 'Truly, truly, I say to you, before Abraham was born, I am'" (v. 58). Unlike many modern deniers of His deity, the Jews knew exactly what He was claiming, as their subsequent attempt to stone Him for blasphemy makes clear (v. 59). In John 13:19 Jesus told His disciples that when what He predicted came to pass, they would believe that He is Yahweh. Even His enemies, coming to arrest Him in Gethsemane, were overwhelmed by His divine power and fell to the ground when Jesus said "I am" (John 18:5–8).

All of the above lines of evidence converge on one inescapable point: Jesus Christ claimed absolute equality with God. Thus He could say, "I and the Father are one" (John 10:30); "He who sees Me sees the One who sent Me" (John 12:45); and "He who has seen Me has seen the Father" (14:9–10).

Those who would deny that Jesus claimed to be God must deny the historical accuracy and truthfulness of the gospel records, and thereby establish themselves as superior sources of truth. They are saying they know more about what was true two thousand years ago than the inspired eyewitnesses. Such skepticism is unwarranted, however, since the New Testament is by far the most well-attested document of the ancient world.[4] Skeptics are also hard-pressed to explain why Jesus' monotheistic Jewish followers would have embraced His deity so early in church history apart from His own claims. William Lane Craig notes,

> Within twenty years of the crucifixion a full-blown Christology proclaiming Jesus as God incarnate existed. How does one explain this worship by monotheistic Jews of one of their countrymen as God incarnate, apart from the claims of Jesus Himself? . . . if Jesus never made any such claims, then the belief of the earliest Christians in this regard becomes inexplicable.[5]

This section affirming our Lord's deity flows directly from the confrontation that arose when Jesus healed a crippled man on the Sabbath (John 5:1–16; see chap. 5). The Lord did not violate the Old Testament Sabbath regulations, but rather the rabbinic additions to those regulations. Yet He did not defend Himself by pointing out the distinction between God's Law and man's extraneous tradition. Instead, He responded in a far more radical way—He maintained that He was equal with God and thus had the right to do whatever He wanted on the Sabbath. The result is one of the most profound Christological discourses in all of Scripture. In verses 17–24 Jesus makes five unmistakable claims to full equality with God: He is equal with the Father in His person, in His works, in His power and sovereignty, in His judgment, and in the honor due Him.

Jesus Is Equal to God in His Person

But He answered them, "My Father is working until now, and I Myself am working." For this reason therefore the Jews were seeking all the more to kill Him, because He not only was breaking the Sabbath, but also was calling God His own Father, making Himself equal with God. (5:17–18)

The Sabbath observance was at the heart of Jewish worship of Jesus' day. The Lord's reply to those who challenged Him for violating it (5:16), "My Father is working until now, and I Myself am working," implies that the Sabbath was not instituted for God's benefit but for man's (Mark 2:27). In other words, the Sabbath restriction on working did not apply to God; He was not required to rest on every seventh day. It is true that at the end of creation week, He "rested on the seventh day from all His work which He had done" (Gen. 2:2). That, however, was not because He was tired, for "the Everlasting God, the LORD, the Creator of the ends of the earth does not become weary or tired" (Isa. 40:28). Instead, it was to set a divine example for man to rest one day out of each week (Ex. 20:9–11).[6]

The significance of the seventh day is underscored by the three references to it in Genesis 2:1–3. According to verse 3, God "sanctified" ("set apart"; "separated") that day to distinguish it from the first six, none of which is so designated. Three verbs in the passage, each of them associated with the work of God, reveal why He uniquely set apart the seventh day.

"Completed" (v. 1) stresses that the entire work of God in creation was finished by the end of the sixth day. In contrast to the theory of evolution (whether atheistic or theistic), the Bible denies that the creative process is still ongoing.

Since His work of creation was completed, God "rested" (vv.

2–3). As noted above, that does not imply any weariness on His part (Isa. 40:28); the verb merely indicates that by the seventh day God had ceased to do the work of creation (cf. Ex. 20:11).

Finally, God "blessed" the seventh day (v. 3); that is, He set it aside as a memorial. Every Saturday of every week serves as a reminder that God created the entire universe in six days, and then rested from His creative activity.

But as even the rabbis themselves acknowledged, God's Sabbath rest (cf. Heb. 4:9–10) from His creative work does not obviate His unceasing providential work of sustaining the universe (Heb. 1:3). Jesus' statement that He worked on the Sabbath just like the Father was nothing less than a claim to full deity and equality with God; that "the Son of Man is Lord of the Sabbath" (Matt. 12:8). His words also served as a subtle rebuke of the Jewish legalistic system, under which He had been indicted for doing good and showing mercy on the Sabbath. After all, God Himself does good and shows mercy on the Sabbath. Jesus, therefore, maintained that it is right to do good on the Sabbath, since God does. Ironically, even the unbelieving Jews performed acts of mercy on the Sabbath (cf. 7:23; Luke 14:5)—the very thing for which they hypocritically rebuked Jesus.

The hostile Jewish leaders instantly grasped the import of Jesus' words and as a result "were seeking [the tense of the verb indicates continuous action] all the more to kill Him" (cf. v. 16). He was "not only breaking the Sabbath, but [even worse in their minds, Jesus] also was calling God His own Father, making Himself equal with God" (cf. 10:30–33). In contrast to the Jews' collective reference to God as "our Father," Jesus called God His own Father. The clear implication, which His opponents readily understood, was that He was claiming to be fully equal with God (cf. 1:1; 8:58; 20:28; Phil. 2:6). In response, they intensified their efforts to take His life (cf. 7:1, 19, 25; 8:37, 40, 59; 11:53), not just for exposing their self-styled legalism, but now with justification (in their minds), because He was asserting His deity.

JESUS IS EQUAL TO GOD IN HIS WORKS

Therefore Jesus answered and was saying to them, "Truly, truly, I say to you, the Son can do nothing of Himself, unless it is something He sees the Father doing; for whatever the Father does, these things the Son also does in like manner. For the Father loves the Son, and shows Him all things that He Himself is doing; and the Father will show Him greater works than these, so that you will marvel. (5:19–20)

For a mere man to claim to be God was, to the Jews, an outrageous act of blasphemy. Therefore if they had misunderstood Him, Jesus surely would have immediately and vehemently denied making such a claim (cf. Acts 14:11–15; Rev. 19:10; 22:8–9). But instead, He became even more forceful and emphatic, introducing His next statement with the solemn affirmation, "truly, truly, I say to you." In the strongest possible terms, the Lord assured His hearers that what He said to them was true. He further defended His healing on the Sabbath by tying His activities directly to those of the Father. "The Son can do nothing of Himself," Jesus declared, "unless it is something He sees the Father doing." He always acted in perfect harmony with and subordination to the Father's will. Thus, His works paralleled those of the Father in both their nature and extent, "for whatever the Father does, these things the Son also does in like manner." Of course, only someone who is equal to the Father could do everything that He does. Christ's statement, then, was a clear declaration of His own divinity.

The perfect harmony that characterizes the joint working of the Father and the Son stems from the absolute unity of essence that they share (cf. John 17:21). Because they are one in being—one eternal God (John 10:30)—to see Christ act is to see God act (John 12:45; 14:9–10). By accusing Jesus of wrongdoing, the religious leaders were actually doing what they charged Jesus of doing, impugning the holy nature of God Himself.

In verse 20 Jesus described the oneness of the Father and the Son as a union of love: "The Father loves the Son [cf. 3:35; 17:26; Matt. 3:17; 17:5; 2 Peter 1:17] and shows Him all things that He Himself is doing." The verb translated "loves" is not *agapaō,* the love of will and choice, but *phileō,* the love of deep feelings; the warmth of affection that a father feels for his son. This is the only time in the New Testament that it is used to refer to the Father's love for the Son. The present tense of the verb indicates an eternally uninterrupted and all-knowing love that leaves no room for ignorance, making it is impossible for Jesus to have been unaware of God's will, whether about the Sabbath, or about anything else.

Jesus continued by declaring that the Father would show Him still greater works. His healing of the crippled man had amazed the crowds. But in obedience to the Father, Jesus predicted that He would perform deeds that were even more spectacular—including raising the dead (v. 21) and judging all people (v. 22). As a result, His listeners would marvel.

Jesus Is Equal to God in His Power and Sovereignty

For just as the Father raises the dead and gives them life, even so the Son also gives life to whom He wishes. (5:21)

By asserting His equality with God, Jesus claimed that He had the power to raise the dead "just as the Father raises the dead and gives them life." The Bible teaches that only God has the power to give life to the dead (Deut. 32:39; 1 Sam. 2:6; 2 Kings 5:7; Acts 26:8; 2 Cor. 1:9; Heb. 11:19), and the Old Testament records several instances where He did so (1 Kings 17:17–24; 2 Kings 4:32–37; 13:20–21). Because His power is the same as the Father, Jesus Christ is able to raise the physically dead (11:25–44; Matt. 9:18–25; Luke 7:11–15; cf. John 6:39–40, 44). Moreover, He has the power to give spiritual life to the spiritually dead. "Whoever drinks of the water that I will give him," Jesus promised, "shall never thirst; but the water that I will give him will become in him a well of water springing up to eternal life" (John 4:14). In John 6 He admonished His hearers, "Do not work for the food which perishes, but for the food which endures to eternal life, which the Son of Man will give to you," because He is "the bread of God . . . which comes down out of heaven, and gives life to the world" (vv. 27, 33; cf. vv. 35, 48, 54; 1:4; 10:28; 11:25; 14:6; 17:2).

Unlike Elijah (1 Kings 17:22) and Elisha (2 Kings 4:34–35), Jesus did not merely act as God's representative when He raised the dead, but as God Himself. The Son Himself gives resurrection and spiritual life "to whom He wishes." As God is the source of life, so Jesus Christ is the source of life. As God chooses when He gives life, so does the Son choose, in perfect agreement with the Father, a truth illustrated by the salvation of sinners. All whom the Father chose before the foundation of the world to give to the Son will come to Him, and He will not reject any of them (John 6:37). Even Jesus' truly human prayer in Gethsemane, "My Father, if it is possible, let this cup pass from Me; yet not as I will, but as You will" (Matt. 26:39) yields to the perfect concord between the persons of the Godhead.

JESUS IS EQUAL TO GOD IN HIS JUDGMENT

For not even the Father judges anyone, but He has given all judgment to the Son, (5:22)

Jesus' authority to grant spiritual life to whomever He chooses is consistent with His authority to judge all men on the last day (cf. 3:18–19; 12:48). Since God is the "judge of all the earth" (Gen. 18:25; cf. 1 Sam. 2:10; 1 Chron. 16:33; Pss. 82:8; 94:2; 96:13; 98:9), the fact that the Father judges no one, but "has given all judgment to the Son" further attests to Christ's deity. Because their wills are in perfect harmony, all judgment can be given to Christ in the assurance that His judgment will be, in fact, the very same as the Father's judgment. Although judgment was not the primary purpose of Christ's first coming to earth (3:17; 12:47), it remains the inescapable result of rejecting the salvation He offers (3:18).

In the future, "the Lord Jesus will be revealed from heaven with His mighty angels in flaming fire, dealing out retribution to those who do not know God and to those who do not obey the gospel of our Lord Jesus" (2 Thess. 1:7–8), because God "has fixed a day in which He will judge the world in righteousness through a Man whom He has appointed, having furnished proof to all men by raising Him from the dead" (Acts 17:31). On that final, terrible day of judgment, those who have rejected Jesus will hear Him say, "I never knew you; depart from Me, you who practice lawlessness" (Matt. 7:23).

JESUS IS EQUAL TO GOD IN HIS HONOR

so that all will honor the Son even as they honor the Father. He who does not honor the Son does not honor the Father who sent Him. "Truly, truly, I say to you, he who hears My word, and

believes Him who sent Me, has eternal life, and does not come into judgment, but has passed out of death into life. (5:23–24)

The Father's purpose in entrusting all judgment to Jesus is "so that all will honor the Son even as they honor the Father." It is only fitting that those equal in nature (vv. 17–18), works (vv. 19–20), power and sovereignty (v. 21), and judgment (v. 22) would be accorded equal honor. The Father's honor is not diminished by the honor paid to Christ; on the contrary, it is enhanced.

Although the unbelieving Jews thought they were truly worshiping God while rejecting His Son (cf. 16:2), such was not the case, for "he who does not honor the Son does not honor the Father who sent Him." This was an astounding claim on Jesus' part, as D. A. Carson notes:

> In a theistic universe, such a statement belongs to one who is himself to be addressed as God (cf. 20:28), or to stark insanity. The one who utters such things is to be dismissed with pity or scorn, or worshipped as Lord. If with much current scholarship we retreat to seeing in such material less the claims of the Son than the beliefs and witness of the Evangelist and his church, the same options confront us. Either John is supremely deluded and must be dismissed as a fool, or his witness is true and Jesus is to be ascribed the honours due God alone. There is no rational middle ground.[7]

When He was asked, "What shall we do, so that we may work the works of God?" Jesus answered, "This is the work of God, that you believe in Him whom He has sent" (6:28–29). "He who hates Me," He warned, "hates My Father also" (15:23). Those who refuse to honor the Son while claiming to honor the Father are actually self-deceived. John Heading writes,

> It is not up to a man to decide that he will honour the One or the Other; it is either both or neither. In religious circles, it is too easy for unbelief to contemplate God but not the Son. Knowledge of One implies knowledge of the Other (John 8:19); hatred of One implies hatred of the Other (15:23); denial of the One implies denial of the Other (1 John 2:23).[8]

That the Father and the Son are to be afforded equal honor forcefully asserts Christ's deity and equality with God, who declared through the prophet Isaiah, "I will not give My glory to another" (Isa. 42:8; 48:11). Yet, the Father has commanded that all will honor the Son. In Philippians 2:9–11 Paul wrote,

> For this reason also, God highly exalted Him, and bestowed on Him the name which is above every name, so that at the name of Jesus every knee will bow, of those who are in heaven and on earth and under the earth, and that every tongue will confess that Jesus Christ is Lord, to the glory of God the Father.

Willingly or unwillingly, everyone will eventually obey the Father's command to honor Jesus Christ.

Jesus closed this section of His discourse by reaffirming His authority to give eternal life to whomever He desires. The Lord underscored the statement's monumental significance by introducing it with the solemn formula amēn, amēn (truly, truly). He identified those who receive eternal life as those who hear His word (or message) and believe the Father who sent Him. As always in the

Scriptures, divine sovereignty in salvation does not preclude human responsibility to repent and believe the gospel. The blessed promise to those who believe is that they do "not come into judgment, but [have] passed out of death into life." As Paul wrote to the Romans, "There is now no condemnation for those who are in Christ Jesus" (Rom. 8:1).

The claims of Jesus Christ confront everyone, forcing them to make a decision either for or against Him. There is no neutral ground, for as Jesus said, "He who is not with Me is against Me; and he who does not gather with Me, scatters" (Luke 11:23). Those who accept Him for who He is, God incarnate in human flesh, will be saved from their sins through Him (Matt. 1:21; 1 Tim. 1:15; Heb. 7:25). But those who believe Him to be anything other than who He truly is will one day face His judgment (John 3:18; 9:39; 12:47–48; 16:8–9; Acts 10:38–42; 17:31; 2 Tim. 4:1).

Chapter 9

ONE WITH THE FATHER

JOHN 10:22–42

At that time the Feast of the Dedication took place at Jerusalem; it was winter, and Jesus was walking in the temple in the portico of Solomon. The Jews then gathered around Him, and were saying to Him, "How long will You keep us in suspense? If You are the Christ, tell us plainly." Jesus answered them, "I told you, and you do not believe; the works that I do in My Father's name, these testify of Me. But you do not believe because you are not of My sheep. My sheep hear My voice, and I know them, and they follow Me; and I give eternal life to them, and they will never perish; and no one will snatch them out of My hand. My Father, who has given them to Me, is greater than all; and no one is able to snatch them out of the Father's hand. I and the Father are one." The Jews picked up stones again to stone Him. Jesus answered them, "I showed you many good works from the Father; for which of them are you stoning Me?" The Jews answered Him, "For a good work we do not stone You, but for blasphemy; and because You, being a man, make Yourself out to be God." Jesus answered them, "Has it not been written in your Law, 'I said, you are gods'? If he called them gods, to whom the word of God came (and the Scripture cannot be broken), do you say of Him, whom the Father sanctified and sent into

the world, 'You are blaspheming,' because I said, 'I am the Son of God'? If I do not do the works of My Father, do not believe Me; but if I do them, though you do not believe Me, believe the works, so that you may know and understand that the Father is in Me, and I in the Father." Therefore they were seeking again to seize Him, and He eluded their grasp. And He went away again beyond the Jordan to the place where John was first baptizing, and He was staying there. Many came to Him and were saying, "While John performed no sign, yet everything John said about this man was true." Many believed in Him there. (10:22–42)

This passage marks the end of John's presentation of Christ's public ministry. For more than three years, Jesus had traveled the length and breadth of Israel, preaching the gospel, calling for repentance, confronting hypocritical false religion, instructing His disciples, and performing countless signs and wonders, which confirmed that He was the Messiah. Through both His words and His works, Jesus had clearly demonstrated His deity and equality with God.

But tragically the nation of Israel, led by her religious leaders, rejected the Messiah—just as the Old Testament predicted would happen (cf. Ps. 22:6–8; Isa. 49:7; 50:6; 53:3). At the end of His life, Jesus had a mere handful of genuine followers; the Bible mentions 120 in Jerusalem (Acts 1:15), and several hundred more, probably in Galilee (1 Cor. 15:6; cf. Matt. 28:7, 16). Instead of embracing Him as their long-awaited Redeemer King, the people of Israel "nailed [Him] to a cross by the hands of godless men and put Him to death" (Acts 2:23). The nation's rejection of Jesus is a frequent theme in John's gospel, appearing in each of the first eleven chapters.[1]

In keeping with that theme, in the concluding section of chapter 10, John punctuates the long presentation of our Lord's public ministry (which began in 1:35) with yet another confrontation between Jesus and the Jewish religious leaders. The dialogue between them unfolds in five scenes: the confrontation, the claim, the charge, the challenge, and the consequences.

THE CONFRONTATION

At that time the Feast of the Dedication took place at Jerusalem; it was winter, and Jesus was walking in the temple in the portico of Solomon. The Jews then gathered around Him, and were saying to Him, "How long will You keep us in suspense? If You are the Christ, tell us plainly." (10:22–24)

John's note that it was now the time of the Feast of the Dedication sets the stage for the next episode. There is a gap of approximately two months between verse 21 (which is still set at the time of the Feast of Tabernacles [7:2, 10, 37]) and verse 22. Some commentators think that Jesus left Jerusalem during that two-month period, since verse 22 calls attention to Jerusalem again as the setting for this dialogue. Others believe the Lord remained in the vicinity of Jerusalem, since verse 22 does not say that He went up to Jerusalem—the usual wording for going to the city from another region (e.g., 2:13; 5:1; 11:55; Matt. 20:17–18). Both views, of course, are only speculative, since the Gospels do not say where Jesus was during those two months.

Known today as Hanukkah, or the Feast of Lights (because of the lamps and candles lit in Jewish homes as part of the celebration), the Feast of the Dedication was celebrated on the twenty-fifth day of the Jewish month Chislev (Nov.–Dec.). It was not one of the feasts prescribed in the Old Testament, but originated during the intertestamental period. The feast commemorated the Israelite's victory over the infamous Syrian king Antiochus Epiphanes (175–164 B.C.). A devotee of Greek culture, Antiochus in a decree given by him in 167 B.C., sought to impose that culture on his subjects (a process known as Hellenization). Antiochus captured Jerusalem and desecrated the temple (170 B.C.) by sacrificing a pig on the altar, setting up a pagan altar in its place, and erecting a statue of Zeus in the most holy place. As he attempted to systematically stamp out Judaism, Antiochus brutally oppressed the Jews, who clung tenaciously to their religion. Under his despotic direction, the Jews were required to offer sacrifices to pagan gods; they were not allowed to own or read the Old Testament Scriptures, and copies of it were destroyed. Antiochus was the first pagan king to persecute the Jews for their religion (cf. Dan. 8:9–14, 23–25; 11:21–35).

Antiochus' savage persecution caused the pious Jews to rise in revolt, led by a priest named Mattathias and his sons. After three years of guerilla warfare the Jews, under the brilliant military leadership of Judas Maccabeus (the son of Mattathias), were able to retake Jerusalem. On 25 Chislev 164 B.C., they liberated the temple, rededicated it, and established the Feast of Dedication.

The Feast of Dedication, which celebrated the successful revolt, took place in winter, which may explain why Jesus, who was in the temple, was walking specifically in the portico of Solomon. It probably was cold, and may have been raining, since winter is the rainy season in Palestine. The portico of Solomon would have provided a measure of protection from the elements; it was a roofed colonnade supported by pillars, located on the east side of the temple overlooking the Kidron Valley below. Many people frequented the site, especially in inclement weather. Some walked there to meditate, and rabbis sometimes taught their students there. Later, the early Christians would gather in the portico of Solomon to proclaim the gospel (Acts 3:11; 5:12).

It should be noted that some see in John's reference to winter a veiled reference to the Jews' spiritual state; that it described not only the season of the year, but also Israel's spiritual coldness. "The thoughtful reader of the Gospel understands that time and temperature notations in John are reflections of the spiritual condition of the persons in the stories (cf. 3:2; 13:30; 18:3, 18; 20:1, 19; 21:3–4)."?[2]

The hostile Jewish leaders accosted the Lord (the verb weakly translated "gathered around" literally means "to surround," or "to encircle" [cf. Luke 21:20; Acts 14:20; Heb. 11:30]), and demanded of Him, "How long will You keep us in suspense? If You are the Christ, tell us plainly." By asking Jesus if He was the Messiah, the Jewish leaders were certainly asking the right question; indeed, it is the most significant question anyone can ask (cf. Matt. 16:15–16). But given the revelation they had seen and heard, and their hostility to Jesus over the course of His ministry, their motive was suspect.

Far from being an honest request for information, their inquiry was actually just another attempt to trap Jesus with a view to getting rid of Him. Because He was the greatest threat to their power and prestige, they were desperately looking for a way to discredit Him and dispose of Him altogether. They were unsettled by the miraculous signs He performed (11:47); tired of the divisions He caused (Luke 12:51–53), even within their own ranks (cf. 9:16); fearful of the revolt He might spark against Rome, thereby jeopardizing their privileged political status (11:48); and angered by His public rebuke of their hypocrisy (e.g., Matt. 23:1–36). Most of all, they were outraged by His unapologetic claim to be God (5:18; 10:33; 19:7). The Jewish authorities' strategy was to make Him to declare publicly (the verb translated "plainly" can also be translated "publicly" or "openly" [7:4, 13, 26; 11:54; 18:20]) that He was the Messiah, so that they would have a pretext for arresting Him.

THE CLAIM

Jesus answered them, "I told you, and you do not believe; the works that I do in My Father's name, these testify of Me. But you do not believe because you are not of My sheep. My sheep hear My voice, and I know them, and they follow Me; and I give eternal life to them, and they will never perish; and no one will snatch them out of My hand. My Father, who has given them to Me, is greater than all; and no one is able to snatch them out of the Father's hand. I and the Father are one." The Jews picked up stones again to stone Him. (10:25–31)

But Jesus *had* told them plainly who He was (cf. 5:17ff.; 8:12, 24, 58); in fact, He had spent the last three years doing so. Not only that, the works that He did in the Father's name also demonstrated that He was the Messiah; the Son of God; God in human flesh (cf. vv. 32, 38; 3:2; 5:36; 7:31; 11:47; 14:11; Acts 2:22). The Lord's twice-repeated declaration, "You do not believe," indicates that the problem was not due to any ambiguity on His part, but rather to their spiritual blindness. They lacked understanding, not because they lacked information, but because they lacked repentance and faith. Their unbelief was not due to insufficient exposure to the truth, but to their hatred of the truth and love of sin and lies

(John 3:1–21). Anyone who willingly seeks the truth will find it (7:17), but Jesus refused to commit Himself to those who willfully rejected the truth. Had He given them the plain answer they were demanding, they would not have believed Him anyway (cf. 8:43; Matt. 26:63–65; Luke 22:66–67).

From the perspective of human responsibility, the hostile Jews did not believe because they had deliberately rejected the truth. But from the standpoint of divine sovereignty, they did not believe because they were not of the Lord's sheep, which were given Him by the Father (v. 29; 6:37; 17:2, 6, 9). A full understanding of exactly how those two realities, human responsibility and divine sovereignty, work together lies beyond human comprehension; but there is no difficulty with them in the infinite mind of God. Significantly, the Bible does not attempt to harmonize them, nor does it apologize for the logical tension that stands between them. For example, speaking of Judas Iscariot's treachery, Jesus said in Luke 22:22, "The Son of Man is going [to be betrayed] as it has been determined." In other words, Judas's betrayal of Christ was in accord with God's eternal purpose. But then Jesus added, "Woe to that man by whom He is betrayed!" That Judas's betrayal was part of God's plan did not relieve him of the responsibility for his crime. In Acts 2:23 Peter said that Jesus was "delivered over [to the cross] by the predetermined plan and foreknowledge of God." Yet he also charged Israel with responsibility for having "nailed [Jesus] to a cross by the hands of godless men and put Him to death." God's sovereignty never excuses human sin.

Repeating what He said in His discourse on the Good Shepherd, Jesus said, "My sheep hear My voice, and I know them, and they follow Me." The elect will heed Christ's call to salvation and continue in faith and obedience to eternal glory (cf. Rom. 8:29–30).

The Lord continued by articulating the wonderful truth that those who are His sheep need never fear being lost. "I give eternal life to them," Jesus declared, "and they will never perish; and no one will snatch them out of My hand. My Father, who has given them to Me, is greater than all; and no one is able to snatch them out of the Father's hand." Nowhere in Scripture is there a stronger affirmation of the absolute eternal security of all true Christians. Jesus plainly taught that the security of the believer in salvation does not depend on human effort, but is grounded in the gracious, sovereign election, promise, and power of God.

Christ's words reveal seven realities that bind every true Christian forever to God. *First, believers are His sheep*, and it is the duty of the Good Shepherd to protect His flock. "This is the will of Him who sent Me," Jesus said, "that of all that He has given Me I lose nothing, but raise it up on the last day" (6:39). To insist that a true Christian can somehow be lost is to deny the truth of that statement. It is also to defame the character of the Lord Jesus Christ—making Him out to be an incompetent shepherd, unable to hold on to those entrusted to Him by the Father.

Second, Christ's sheep hear only His voice and follow only Him. Since they will not listen to or follow a stranger (10:5), they could not possibly wander away from Him and be eternally lost.

Third, Christ's sheep have eternal life. To speak of eternal life somehow ending is a contradiction in terms.

Fourth, Christ gives eternal life to His sheep. Since they did nothing to earn it, they can do nothing to lose it.

Fifth, Christ promised that His sheep will never perish. Were even one to do so, it would make Him a liar.

Sixth, no one—not false shepherds (the thieves and robbers of verse 1), false prophets (symbolized by the wolf of verse 12), nor even the devil himself—*is powerful enough to snatch Christ's sheep out of His hand.*

Finally, Christ's sheep are held not only in His hand, but also in the hand of the Father, who is greater than all; and thus no one is able to snatch them out of His hand either. Infinitely secure, the believer's "life is hidden with Christ in God" (Col. 3:3).

The Father and the Son jointly guarantee the eternal security of believers because, as Jesus declared, "I and the Father are one" (the Greek word "one" is neuter, not masculine; it speaks of "one substance," not "one person"). Thus their unity of purpose and action in safeguarding believers is undergirded by their unity of nature and essence. The whole matter of security is summarized in our Lord's own words in John 6:39–40:

> This is the will of Him who sent Me, that of all that He has given Me I lose nothing, but raise it up on the last day. For this is the will of My Father, that everyone who beholds the Son and believes in Him will have eternal life, and I Myself will raise him up on the last day.

Incensed by what they accurately and unmistakably perceived as another claim to deity by Jesus, the Jews, self-righteously exploding in a fit of passion, picked up stones again to stone Him—the fourth time in John's gospel that they had attempted to kill Him (5:16–18; 7:1; 8:59). Though the Romans had withheld the right of capital punishment from the Jews (18:31), this angry lynch mob was ready to take matters into its own hands.

The Charge

Jesus answered them, "I showed you many good works from the Father; for which of them are you stoning Me?" The Jews

answered Him, "For a good work we do not stone You, but for blasphemy; and because You, being a man, make Yourself out to be God." (10:32–33)

Showing majestic calm in the face of His opponents' murderous rage, Jesus asked them pointedly, "I showed you many good [the adjective *kalos* means "noble," "excellent," or "beautiful"] works from the Father; for which of them are you stoning Me?" The Lord did not soften or withdraw His claim to be equal with God. Instead, He forced them to face and deal with His miraculous good works done at the direction of the Father (cf. 5:19–23). Those works offered visible, tangible proof of His oneness with God (cf. 5:36), and thus proved that He was not a blasphemer, as in fact His opponents were. The Lord's question also put the Jewish leaders in the awkward position of opposing the very public and popular good things He had done in healing the sick, feeding the hungry, liberating the demon-possessed, and even raising the dead (cf. Luke 7:14–15; 8:52–56; John 11).

But the enraged Jews were not deterred by any miracles. Unlike the formerly blind man, who had drawn the proper conclusion from Jesus' miraculous deeds (cf. 9:33), the angry mob simply brushed His works aside. They answered Him, "For a good work we do not stone You, but for blasphemy; and because You, being a man, make Yourself out to be God." As noted above, the signs Jesus' performed demonstrated His oneness with the Father, and proved that He was not guilty of blasphemy. But the Lord's appeal to His mighty works was lost on those in the crowd. Their minds were made up, and their love of sin held them captive to Satan, death, and judgment.

In contrast to those who deny that Christ ever actually claimed to be God, the hostile Jews understood perfectly that He was saying exactly that. But they refused to consider the possibility that His claim might be true. In their minds, Jesus was guilty of the ultimate act of blasphemy because, as they told Him, "You, being a man, make Yourself out to be God." As was the case with Jesus' earlier claims to deity, their ultimate reaction was a plot to kill Him (5:16-18; 8:58-59). Ironically, their charge was the reverse of the truth. Far from being a mere man who was arrogantly promoting himself as God, Jesus was in fact almighty God who had selflessly humbled Himself in becoming a man to die for the world (1:14; cf. Phil. 2:5-11).

THE CHALLENGE

Jesus answered them, "Has it not been written in your Law, 'I said, you are gods'? If he called them gods, to whom the word of God came (and the Scripture cannot be broken), do you say of Him, whom the Father sanctified and sent into the world, 'You are blaspheming,' because I said, 'I am the Son of God'? If I do not do the works of My Father, do not believe Me; but if I do them, though you do not believe Me, believe the works, so that you may know and understand that the Father is in Me, and I in the Father." (10:34-38)

It is important to note that Jesus, having been charged with blasphemy, did not claim that His opponents had misunderstood Him. His refusal to do so makes it clear that His declaration, "I and the Father are one" (v. 30) was in fact what they knew it to be, a claim to be God.

Jesus knew how seriously they took the very word "God," so He addressed that one matter by quoting a passage from the Old

Testament: "Has it not been written in your Law, 'I said, you are gods'? If he called them gods, to whom the word of God came (and the Scripture cannot be broken), do you say of Him, whom the Father sanctified and sent into the world, 'You are blaspheming,' because I said, 'I am the Son of God'?" The very Law—a reference here to the entire Old Testament, not just the Pentateuch—that the Jews prized so highly used the term "gods" to refer to others than God Himself. The reference is to Psalm 82:6, where God rebuked Israel's unjust judges, calling them "gods" (in a far lesser sense) because they ruled as His representatives and spokesmen (cf. Ex. 4:16; 7:1). The Jewish leaders could not dispute the fact that those judges were called "gods," because the Scripture cannot be broken—a clear and unambiguous declaration of the absolute authority and inerrancy of the Bible. Scripture can never be nullified or set aside, though the Jews often tried (cf. Mark 7:13).

Since God called the unjust judges "gods," Jesus' argument ran, how could His opponents "say of Him, whom the Father sanctified and sent into the world, 'You are blaspheming,' because He said, 'I am the Son of God'?" If mere men, who were evil, could in some sense be called gods, how could it be inappropriate for Jesus, the one whom the Father sanctified and sent into the world, to call Himself the Son of God (cf. 5:19–27)? The point is not to add to the evidence of His deity; it is simply a rebuke on the level of their overreaction to use of the word "God" in reference to Jesus. He had proven that He was entitled to that title in the full divine sense, as He would affirm again in verses 37–38. They were merely those to whom the word of God came; Jesus was the Incarnate Word of God (1:1, 14). As one commentator further explains,

This passage is sometimes misinterpreted as though Jesus was simply classing himself with men in general. He appeals to the psalm that speaks of men as "gods," so runs the reasoning, and thus justifies his speaking of himself as Son of God. He is "god" in the same sense as others. But this is not taking seriously enough what Jesus actually says. He is arguing from the less to the greater. If the word *god* could be used of people who were no more than judges, how much more could it be used of one with greater dignity, greater importance and significance than any mere judge, one "whom the Father sanctified and sent into the world"? He is not placing himself on a level with men, but setting himself apart from them.[3]

The Lord's appeal to the Old Testament was a challenge for the Jewish leaders to abandon their biased conclusions about Him and consider the objective evidence. In that same vein Jesus continued by saying, "If I do not do the works of My Father, do not believe Me; but if I do them, though you do not believe Me, believe the works, so that you may know and understand that the Father is in Me, and I in the Father." As He had so many other times before (cf. vv. 25, 32; 5:19–20, 36; 14:10–11), the Lord appealed to His works as proof of His indivisible union with the Father (v. 30). But incredibly, the religious leaders of Israel were so spiritually blind that they could not recognize God's works. If Jesus did not do the works of the Father, they would have been right in refusing to believe Him. On the other hand, because He did do them, they should have put aside their reluctance to believe His words, and chosen instead to believe the clear testimony of His works. As supposed men of God, they should have been willing to follow the evidence to its logical conclusion.

The Consequences

Therefore they were seeking again to seize Him, and He eluded their grasp. And He went away again beyond the Jordan to the place where John was first baptizing, and He was staying there. Many came to Him and were saying, "While John performed no sign, yet everything John said about this man was true." Many believed in Him there. (10:39–42)

Not unexpectedly, the Lord's challenge to His opponents fell on deaf ears. Instead of objectively considering the evidence, the Jewish leaders responded as they had before by seeking again to seize Him. It may be that they were planning to haul Him out of the temple before stoning Him (cf. Acts 21:30–32), but more likely they meant to arrest Him and hold Him for trial before the Sanhedrin. No matter what they intended, His hour still had not come (7:30; 8:20), so Jesus eluded their grasp. He left Jerusalem, not to return until three or four months later to raise Lazarus from the dead (John 11:1ff.) and enter Jerusalem in triumph (12:12ff.).

But as always, there were some who believed and embraced Him (cf. vv. 19–21; 7:12, 43; 9:16). After leaving Jerusalem, the Lord "went away again beyond the Jordan to the place where John was first baptizing" (Bethany beyond the Jordan). While He "was staying there many came to Him and were saying, 'While John performed no sign, yet everything John said about this man was true.'" The people there remembered Him and came to Him as they had earlier flocked to John the Baptist. While John performed no sign, he was nonetheless the preeminent witness to Jesus; as the people noted, "Everything John said about Him was true." Not surprisingly, many believed in Him there.

So Jesus' public ministry closed with one last rejection by the very leaders who should have hailed Him as the Messiah. Their rejection foreshadowed His ultimate rejection a few months later, when the people, under their influence (Matt. 27:20), "cried out, 'Away with Him, away with Him, crucify Him!'" (John 19:15).

Even today, there are many who, like the hostile Jewish leaders, allow their preconceived ideas about religion and their love for sin to blind them to the saving truth about Jesus Christ. Nonetheless those who are drawn to Him in repentance and faith will come to know the truth of who He is (John 7:17). To them will be given "the right to become children of God, even to those who believe in His name" (John 1:12).

———∙∞∙———

Chapter 10

THE GREAT I AM

Selected Passages from John

Throughout the gospel of John, Jesus repeatedly used the phrase "I am" to illustrate specific aspects of His saving work. He described Himself as "the bread of life" (John 6:48), "the Light of the world" (8:12), "the door of the sheep" (10:7, 9), "the good shepherd" (10:11, 14), "the resurrection and the life" (11:25), "the way, and the truth, and the life" (14:6), and "the true vine" (15:1, 5). In other passages, He used "I am" in an absolute, unqualified sense (4:26; 8:24, 28, 58; 13:19; 18:5–8), to appropriate for Himself the Old Testament name of God (Ex. 3:14).

In claiming the title "I am," Jesus was claiming nothing less than full equality with God. A survey of key passages from John's gospel demonstrates the profound truth encompassed in Jesus' "I am" statements: Jesus is God in the flesh, the Immanuel prophesied in Isaiah 7:14 and declared in Matthew 1:20–23.

I Am the Bread of Life

Jesus said to them, "I am the bread of life; he who comes to Me will not hunger, and he who believes in Me will never thirst. (John 6:35)

I am the bread of life. (6:48)

The people's dullness and lack of understanding prompted Jesus to declare plainly to them, "I am the bread of life." The Lord had not been referring to actual bread, as they mistakenly thought, but to Himself; He is the very bread He earlier promised to give (v. 27). No physical bread, not even manna nor the bread Jesus had just created the evening before (6:1–13), could permanently cure physical hunger. Thus, when the Lord declared that those who come to Him will never again hunger or thirst, He was speaking not of the body, but of the soul. Here, as in Matthew 5:6, the human need to know God is expressed metaphorically as hungering and thirsting (cf. Ps. 42:1–2; 63:1).

Two simple verbs in John 6:35 define man's part in the salvation process: "comes" and "believes." To come to Christ is to forsake the old life of sin and rebellion and submit to Him as Lord. Though John does not use the term "repentance" in his gospel, the concept is clearly implied in the idea of coming to Christ (cf. 1 Thess. 1:9). As Charles Spurgeon put it, "You and your sins must separate, or you and your God will never come together."[1] To believe in Christ is to trust completely in Him as the Messiah and Son of God, and to acknowledge that salvation comes solely through faith in Him (14:6; Acts 4:12). Repentance and faith are two sides of the same coin; to repent is to turn from sin, and to believe is to turn to the Savior. They are inseparable.

I Am the Light of the World

Then Jesus again spoke to them, saying, "I am the Light of the world; he who follows Me will not walk in the darkness, but will have the Light of life." (8:12)

While I am in the world, I am the Light of the world." (9:5)

Earlier in his gospel, John had already used the metaphor of light to describe Jesus (1:4, 8–9; cf. Rev. 21:23), and it was one rich in Old Testament allusions (cf. Ex. 13:21–22; 14:19–20; Neh. 9:12, 19; Pss. 27:1; 36:9; 43:3; 44:3; 104:2; 119:105, 130; Prov. 6:23; Isa. 60:19–20; Ezek. 1:4, 13, 26–28; Mic. 7:8; Hab. 3:3–4; Zech. 14:5b–7). By claiming to be the light of the world Jesus was clearly claiming to be God (cf. Ps. 27:1; Isa. 60:19; 1 John 1:5) and to be Israel's Messiah, sent by God to be a "light to the nations" (Isa. 42:6; cf. 49:6; Mal. 4:2).

Jesus Christ alone brings the light of salvation to a sin-cursed world. To the darkness of falsehood He is the light of truth; to the darkness of ignorance He is the light of wisdom; to the darkness of sin He is the light of holiness; to the darkness of sorrow He is the light of joy; and to the darkness of death He is the light of life.

The analogy of light, as with Jesus' earlier use of the metaphor of living water (7:37–38), was particularly relevant to the Feast of Tabernacles. The daily water-pouring ceremony had its nightly counterpart in a lamp-lighting ceremony. In the very Court of the Women where Jesus was speaking, four huge candelabra were lit. So brilliant was their light that one ancient Jewish source declared, "There was not a courtyard in Jerusalem that did not reflect [their] light."[2] The brilliant lights served as a reminder of the pillar of fire by which God had guided Israel in the wilderness (Ex. 13:21–22). The people—even the most dignified leaders—danced exuberantly around the candelabra through the night, holding blazing torches in their hands and singing songs of praise. It was against the backdrop of that ceremony that Jesus made the stunning announcement that He is the true Light of the world.

But unlike the stationary candelabra, Jesus is a light that never goes out and a light to be followed. Just as Israel followed the pillar of fire in the wilderness (Ex. 40:36–38), so Jesus called men to follow Him (1:43; 10:4, 27; 12:26; 21:19, 22; Matt. 4:19; 8:22; 9:9; 10:38; 16:24; 19:21). The one who follows Him, Jesus promised, will not walk in the darkness of sin, the world, and Satan, but will have the Light that produces spiritual life (cf. 1:4; Pss. 27:1; 36:9; Isa. 49:6; Acts 13:47; 2 Cor. 4:4–6; Eph. 5:14; 1 John 1:7). Having been illumined by Jesus, believers reflect His light in the dark world (Matt. 5:14; Eph. 5:8; Phil. 2:15; 1 Thess. 5:5); "They, having kindled their torches at His bright flame, show to the world something of His light."[3]

The word "follows" (*akoloutheō*) is sometimes used in a general sense to speak of the crowds who followed Jesus (e.g., 6:2; Matt. 4:25; 8:1; 12:15; Mark 2:15; 3:7; Luke 7:9; 9:11). But it can also refer, more specifically, to following Him as a disciple (e.g., 1:43; 10:4, 27; 12:26; Matt. 4:20, 22; 9:9; 10:38; 16:24; 19:27; Mark 9:38). In that context, it has the connotation of complete submission to Jesus as Lord. God does not accept a halfhearted following of Christ—of receiving Him as Savior, but not following Him as Lord. The person who comes to Jesus comes to Him on His terms, or he does not come at all (cf. Matt. 8:18–22). Though it requires self-denial and whole-hearted commitment (Matt. 16:24–26), following Christ is not burdensome, since walking in the light is far easier than stumbling around in the dark (cf. Jer. 13:16).

Unless You Believe That I Am He

He was saying to them, "You are from below, I am from above; you are of this world, I am not of this world. Therefore I said to you that you will die in your sins; for unless you believe that

I am He, you will die in your sins." (8:23–24; cf. John 4:25–26; 8:28; 13:18–19)

In these verses, Jesus declared that those who reject Him will die in their sins because they refuse to believe "that I am He." The Lord's use of the absolute, unqualified phrase "I am" (as mentioned earlier, the pronoun "He" does not appear in the Greek text) is nothing less than a direct claim to full deity. When Moses asked God His name, He replied, "I AM WHO I AM" (Ex. 3:14). In the Septuagint (the Greek translation of the Old Testament), that is the same phrase (*egō eimi*) Jesus used here. (The Septuagint similarly uses *egō eimi* of God in Deut. 32:39; Isa. 41:4; 43:10, 25; 45:18; 46:4.) Jesus was applying to Himself the tetragrammaton (YHWH, often transliterated as Yahweh)—the name of God that was so sacred that the Jews refused to pronounce it. Unlike many modern cultic groups (such as the Jehovah's Witnesses), the Jews of Jesus' day understood perfectly that He was claiming to be God. In fact, they were so shocked by His use of that name, in reference to Himself (cf. vv. 28, 58), that they attempted to stone Him for blasphemy (v. 59).

Unmistakably, the Lord Himself says that those who reject Him cannot be saved, but will die in their sins. To be a Christian one must believe the full biblical revelation about Jesus: that He is the eternal second person of the Trinity, that He entered space and time as God incarnate, that He was born of a virgin, that He lived a sinless life, that His death on the cross is the only sufficient, substitutionary sacrifice for the sins of all who would ever believe in Him, that He rose from the dead and ascended to the Father in heaven, that He now intercedes for His own redeemed people, and that He will one day return in glory. To reject those truths about

Him is to "be led astray from the simplicity and purity of devotion to Christ" (2 Cor. 11:3), to worship "another Jesus" (v. 4), to be cursed by God (Gal. 1:8–9), and ultimately to hear the Lord say, "I never knew you; depart from Me, you who practice lawlessness" (Matt. 7:23).

The word "unless" introduces the only hope of escape from God's wrath and judgment on sin. R. C. H. Lenski notes,

> The sins of these men will destroy them by robbing them of life eternal only if they refuse to believe in Jesus. The "if" clause [in the KJV] is pure gospel, extending its blessed invitation anew. Yet it is again combined with the warning about dying in sins. This note of warning with its terrifying threat persists because these Jews had chosen the course of unbelief. Yet the "if" opens the door of life in the wall of sin.[4]

Persistent unwillingness to believe the truth about Jesus Christ, by its very nature, precludes the possibility of forgiveness, since salvation comes only through faith in Him (3:15–16, 36; 6:40, 47; Acts 16:31; Rom. 10:9–10; Gal. 3:26; 1 John 5:10–13). Those who continue in unbelief, refusing to embrace in faith all that Jesus is and has done, will die in their sins and be lost forever (cf. 3:18, 36; Heb. 2:3). And apart from the knowledge of the gospel of Jesus Christ, no one can be saved. Therefore believers are commanded to go to the world and preach Christ to everyone (Mark 16:15–16; Luke 24:47; Acts 1:8).

"Before Abraham Was Born, I Am"

So the Jews said to Him, "You are not yet fifty years old, and have You seen Abraham?" Jesus said to them, "Truly, truly, I say

to you, before Abraham was born, I am." Therefore they picked up stones to throw at Him, but Jesus hid Himself and went out of the temple. (8:57–59)

Stubbornly persisting in their misunderstanding of Jesus' words, the Jewish leaders said to Him, "You are not yet fifty years old, and have You seen Abraham?" Abraham had lived more than two millennia earlier; Jesus could not possibly have seen him. They also twisted His words; the Lord had not said that He had seen Abraham, but that Abraham had (prophetically) seen Him (v. 56). It should be noted that the Jews' statement that Jesus was not yet fifty years old does not specify Jesus' exact age, but rather places an upper limit on it. The Lord would have only been in His early thirties, since He was about thirty when He began His ministry (Luke 3:23).

Jesus' solemn reply, "Truly, truly, I say to you, before Abraham was born, I am," was nothing less than a claim to full deity. The Lord once again took for Himself the sacred name of God. Obviously, as the eternal God (John 1:1–2), He existed before Abraham's time. Homer Kent explains, "By using the timeless "I am" rather than "I was," Jesus conveyed not only the idea of existence prior to Abraham, but timelessness—the very nature of God himself (Exod. 3:14)."[5]

The Jewish leaders understood Jesus' claim perfectly. In response, their hatred flamed into violence. Infuriated by what they perceived as blasphemy (cf. 10:33), they took the law into their own hands and picked up stones to throw at Him (cf. Lev. 24:16).

Here is the grip of unbelief so powerful that in the face of irrefutable evidence they were unwilling to accept that as God in human flesh, Jesus was incapable of committing blasphemy; rather all of His claims, no matter how astonishing, were absolutely true. How ironic that the Jewish religious leaders, seemingly so passionate for God's honor that they were ready to cast stones at a blasphemer, were in fact accusing God Himself of blaspheming God.

Significantly, the Lord did not protest that He had been misunderstood. Clearly, He was claiming to be God. Since His hour to die had not yet come (John 7:30; 8:20; 13:1), Jesus would not allow Himself to be killed, but supernaturally hid Himself and went out of the temple (cf. Luke 4:30).

As on this occasion, so it always is that there are only two possible responses to Jesus' claims. One is to accept them as true, and bow before Him in humble, repentant faith, confessing Him as Savior and Lord. The other response, illustrated by Jesus' opponents in this passage, is that of hardened, bitter rejection. The tragic, fearful result of that response will be eternal damnation in hell. As Jesus soberly warned, "Therefore I said to you that you will die in your sins; for unless you believe that I am He, you will die in your sins" (8:24).

I Am the Door to the Sheep

So Jesus said to them again, "Truly, truly, I say to you, I am the door of the sheep. All who came before Me are thieves and robbers, but the sheep did not hear them. I am the door; if anyone enters through Me, he will be saved, and will go in and out and find pasture. The thief comes only to steal and kill and destroy; I came that they may have life, and have it abundantly." (10:7–10)

Since the religious leaders had failed to understand His first figure of speech (regarding the shepherd in vv. 1–6), Jesus said to them again, "Truly, truly, I say to you, I am the door of the sheep."

Sometimes the shepherd slept in the opening of the sheepfold to guard the sheep. No one could enter or leave except through him. In Jesus' metaphor He is the door through which the sheep enter the safety of God's fold and go out to the rich pasture of His blessing. It is through Him that lost sinners can approach the Father and appropriate the salvation He provides; Jesus alone is "the way, and the truth, and the life; no one comes to the Father but through [Him]" (14:6; cf. Acts 4:12; 1 Cor. 3:11; 1 Tim. 2:5). Only Jesus is the true source of the knowledge of God and salvation, and the basis for spiritual security.

The Lord's assertion, "All who came before Me are thieves and robbers," does not, of course, include Israel's true spiritual leaders (such as Moses, Joshua, David, Solomon, Ezra, Nehemiah, Isaiah, Jeremiah, Ezekiel, and Daniel, among many others). Jesus was referring to Israel's false shepherds—her wicked kings, corrupt priests, false prophets, and pseudo-messiahs. However, the true sheep did not hear them; they did not heed them and were not led astray by them (cf. v. 4).

Then Jesus reiterated the vital truth of verse 7: "I am the door;" and added the promise, "If anyone enters through Me, he will be saved." Christ's sheep will experience God's love, care, and protection; they will go in and out freely, not fearing any harm or danger. They will find satisfying pasture as the Lord feeds them (cf. Ezek. 34:15) on His Word (cf. Acts 20:32). In utter contrast to the thieving false shepherds, who came only to steal and kill and destroy the sheep, Jesus came "that they may have life, and have it abundantly." The word "abundantly" (*perissos*) describes something that goes far beyond what is necessary. The matchless gift of the Lord Jesus Christ exceeds all expectation (Rom. 8:32; 2 Cor. 9:15).

I Am The Good Shepherd

I am the good shepherd; the good shepherd lays down His life for the sheep. He who is a hired hand, and not a shepherd, who is not the owner of the sheep, sees the wolf coming, and leaves the sheep and flees, and the wolf snatches them and scatters them. He flees because he is a hired hand and is not concerned about the sheep. I am the good shepherd, and I know My own and My own know Me, even as the Father knows Me and I know the Father; and I lay down My life for the sheep. (10:11–15)

Jesus' identification of Himself as the good shepherd points back to the true shepherd described in verses 2 to 5. The Greek text literally reads, "the shepherd, the good one," setting Christ the Good Shepherd apart from all other shepherds. The Greek term *kalos* (translated "good") refers to His noble character (cf. 1 Tim. 3:7; 4:6; 2 Tim. 2:3; 1 Peter 4:10); He is the perfect, authentic Shepherd; in a class by Himself; preeminent above all others.

Being a faithful shepherd entailed a willingness to lay one's life on the line to protect the sheep. Robbers, and wild animals such as wolves, lions, and bears, were a constant danger (cf. 1 Sam. 17:34; Isa. 31:4; Amos 3:12). But Jesus, the good shepherd, went far beyond merely being willing to risk His life for His sheep; He actually laid down His life for them (cf. v. 15; 6:51; 11:50–51; 18:14). The phrase "lays down His life" is unique to John's writings and always refers to a voluntary, sacrificial death (vv. 15, 17, 18; 13:37–38; 15:13; 1 John 3:16). Jesus gave His life for His sheep, so that they might become part of His flock. The preposition "for" (*huper*) is frequently used in the New Testament to refer to Christ's substitutionary atonement for the elect (cf. v. 15; 6:51; 11:50, 51; 18:14; Luke 22:19; Heb. 2:9; 1 Peter 2:21; 3:18; 1 John 3:16 and throughout Paul's epistles[6]). His death was an actual atonement to provide propitiation for the sins of all who would believe, as they were called and regenerated by the Spirit, because they were chosen by the Father.

Opposite the Good Shepherd, who gives His life for the sheep, is "he who is a hired hand, and not a shepherd, who is not the owner of the sheep, [who] sees the wolf coming [cf. Matt. 7:15; Acts 20:29], and leaves the sheep and flees, and the wolf snatches them and scatters them" (cf. Matt. 9:36; Mark 6:34). The hired hand symbolizes the Jewish religious leaders and, by extension, all false shepherds. They are mercenaries, doing ministry not for love of the souls of men or even love for the truth, but for money (Titus 1:10–11; 1 Peter 5:2; 2 Peter 2:3). Therefore they flee at the first sign of threat to their well-being, because they are not concerned about the sheep. Their overriding priority is self-preservation, and they are unwilling to sacrifice themselves for anyone.

By contrast, the good shepherd knows and cares for his sheep. He loves His own, which is why He gave His life for them. The word "know" is often used in Scripture to denote that love relationship. In Genesis 4:1, 17, 25; 19:8; 24:16; 1 Samuel 1:19, the term "know" describes the intimate love relationship between husband and wife (the NASB translates the Hebrew verb "to know" in those verses as "had relations with"). In Amos 3:2 God said of Israel, "You only have I known of all the families of the earth" (NKJV), speaking not as if He were unaware of any other nations, but of His unique love relationship with His people. Matthew 1:25 literally reads that Joseph "was not knowing [Mary]" until after the birth of Jesus. On the day of judgment, Jesus will send unbelievers away from Him because He does not know them; that is, He has no love relationship with them (Matt. 7:23). In these verses, "know" has that same connotation of a relationship of love. The simple truth here is that Jesus in love knows His own, they in love know Him, the Father in love knows Jesus, and He in love knows the Father. Believers are caught up in the deep and intimate affection that is shared between God the Father and the Lord Jesus Christ (cf. 14:21, 23; 15:10).

I AM THE RESURRECTION AND THE LIFE

Jesus said to her, "I am the resurrection and the life; he who believes in Me will live even if he dies, and everyone who lives and believes in Me will never die. Do you believe this?" (11:25–26)

These verses record part of the conversation between Jesus and Martha, four days after the death of Martha's brother, Lazarus, and just moments before Jesus would raise him from the dead.

Challenging Martha to move beyond an abstract belief in the final resurrection to complete faith in Him, Jesus said to her, "I am the resurrection and the life." Martha's focus was on the end of the age, but time is no obstacle for the one who has the power of resurrection and life (cf. 5:21, 26). Jesus will raise the dead in the future resurrection of which Martha spoke. But He was also going to raise her brother immediately. The Lord called her to a personal trust in Him as the One who alone has power over death.

Jesus' next two statements, "He who believes in Me will live even if he dies, and everyone who lives and believes in Me will never die," are not redundant, as some believe. They teach separate, though related, truths. The one who believes in Jesus will live even if he dies physically because He will raise him on the last day (5:21, 25–29; 6:39–40, 44, 54). And since everyone who lives and believes in Him has eternal life (3:36; 5:24; 6:47, 54), they will never die spiritually (cf. 8:51), since eternal life cannot be extinguished by physical death. As a result, all who trust in Christ can exult, "O death, where is your victory? O death, where is your sting?" (1 Cor. 15:55).

When Jesus challenged Martha, "Do you believe this?" He was not asking her if she believed that He was about to raise her brother. The Lord was calling her to personally believe that He alone was the source of resurrection power and eternal life. Lenski writes,

> To believe "this" is to believe what he says of himself and thus to believe "in him." It is one thing to hear it, to reason and to argue about it; and quite another thing to believe, embrace, trust it. To believe is to receive, hold, enjoy the reality and the power of it, with all that lies in it of joy, comfort, peace, and hope. The measure of our believing, while it is not the measure of our possessing, since the smallest faith has Jesus, the resurrection and the life, completely, is yet the measure of our enjoyment of it all.[7]

Because of His infinite care for Martha's soul, Jesus pointed her to the only source of spiritual life and well-being—Himself.

Martha's affirmation of faith in Jesus stands with the other great confessions of His identity in the Gospels (1:49; 6:69; Matt. 14:33; 16:16). It anticipates John's purpose statement for writing his gospel: "These have been written so that you may believe that Jesus is the Christ, the Son of God; and that believing you may have life in His name" (20:31). Martha emphatically (the Greek text has the personal pronoun in addition to the verb) declared three vital truths about Jesus: Like Andrew (1:41), she confessed that He was the Christ, or Messiah; like John the Baptist (1:34), Nathanael (1:49), and the disciples (Matt. 14:33) she affirmed that He was the Son of God; and finally, like the Old Testament had predicted (cf. Isa. 9:6;

Mic. 5:2), she referred to Him as "He who comes into the world"—the deliverer sent by God (Luke 7:19–20; cf. John 1:9; 3:31; 6:14).

I Am the Way, the Truth, and the Life

Jesus said to him, "I am the way, and the truth, and the life; no one comes to the Father but through Me. (14:6)

As His words clearly demonstrate, Jesus alone is the way to God because He alone is the truth (John 1:14, 17; 18:37; Rev. 3:7; 19:11) about God and He alone possesses the life of God (John 1:4; 5:26; 11:25; 1 John 1:1; 5:20). The Bible teaches that God may be approached exclusively through His only-begotten Son. Jesus alone is the "door of the sheep" (10:7); all others are "thieves and robbers" (v. 8), and it is only the one who "enters through [Him who] will be saved" (v. 9). The way of salvation is a narrow path entered through a small, narrow gate, and few find it (Matt. 7:13–14; cf. Luke 13:24). "There is salvation in no one else," Peter boldly affirmed, "for there is no other name under heaven that has been given among men by which we must be saved" (Acts 4:12). Thus, it is "he who believes in the Son [who] has eternal life; but he who does not obey the Son will not see life, but the wrath of God abides on him" (John 3:36), and "no man can lay a foundation other than the one which is laid, which is Jesus Christ" (1 Cor. 3:11), because "there is one God, and one mediator also between God and men, the man Christ Jesus" (1 Tim. 2:5).

The postmodern belief that there are many paths to religious truth is a satanic lie. F. F. Bruce writes,

He [Jesus] is, in fact, the only way by which men and women may come to the Father; there is no other way. If this seems offensively exclusive, let it be borne in mind that the one who makes this claim is the incarnate Word, the revealer of the Father. If God has no avenue of communication with mankind apart from his Word . . . mankind has no avenue of approach to God apart from that same Word, who became flesh and dwelt among us in order to supply such an avenue of approach.[8]

Jesus alone reveals God (John 1:18; cf. 3:13; 10:30–38; 12:45; 14:9; Col. 1:15, 19; 2:9; Heb. 1:3), and no one who rejects His proclamation of the truth can legitimately claim to know God (John 5:23; 8:42–45; 15:23; Matt. 11:27; 1 John 2:23; 2 John 1:9). It was because the early Christians taught that Jesus Christ is the only way to salvation that Christianity became known as "The Way" (Acts 9:2; 19:9, 23; 22:4; 24:14, 22).

I Am the True Vine

"I am the true vine, and My Father is the vinedresser. . . . I am the vine, you are the branches; he who abides in Me and I in him, he bears much fruit, for apart from Me you can do nothing. (15:1, 5)

Jesus presented this analogy to His disciples in the Upper Room on the night before His death. It was a time of intense drama. One of the twelve men closest to Him, Judas Iscariot, had revealed himself to be a traitor. By this time, Judas had already left to sell out the Lord to the Jewish authorities and set in motion the events leading to Jesus' arrest and murder (13:26–30). The Lord and the remaining eleven disciples would soon leave the upper room for Gethsemane, where Christ would agonize in prayer to the Father, and then be taken prisoner.

The central truth the Lord wanted to communicate in this analogy is the importance of abiding in Him (vv. 4–7, 9–10). In the most basic sense, whether or not individuals abides in Christ reveals whether they are saved (vv. 2, 6). It must be noted that this simple and obvious premise rescues the text from many unnecessary misinterpretations. And it is only to the degree the redeemed abide in Christ that they can bear spiritual fruit.

The verb "abide" (*menō*) describes something that remains where it is, continues in a fixed state, or endures. In this context the word refers to maintaining an unbroken communion with Jesus Christ. The Lord's command, "Abide in Me" (v. 4) is primarily a plea to false disciples of Christ to repent and express true faith in Him. It is also serves to encourage genuine believers to abide in Him in the fullest, deepest, most complete sense.

Always the master storyteller, Jesus wove all the key figures of that night's events into His analogy: He is the vine, the Father the vinedresser, the abiding branches represent the eleven and all other true disciples, and the non-abiding branches picture Judas and all other false disciples like him. One last time before His death Jesus warned against following the pattern of Judas. He challenged all who claim to believe in Him to demonstrate the genuineness of that claim by their enduring faith in Him.

Spoken just hours before His death, Jesus' statement "I am the true vine" affirms His deity (as do the other "I am" statements recorded in John's gospel—6:35; 8:12; 10:7, 9, 11, 14; 11:25; 14:6; cf. 8:24, 28, 58; 13:19; 18:5–6). As God in human flesh, Jesus rightly pointed to Himself as the Source of spiritual life, vitality, growth, and productivity.

The word "true" (*alēthinos*) refers to what is real as distinct from a type (cf. Heb. 8:2; 9:24), perfect as distinct from the imperfect, or genuine as distinct from what is counterfeit (cf. 1 Thess. 1:9; 1 John 5:20; Rev. 3:7, 14; 6:10; 19:11). Jesus is the true vine in the same sense that He is the true light (John 1:9), the final and complete revelation of spiritual truth, and the true bread out of heaven (John 6:32), the final and only source of spiritual sustenance.

THE GREAT I AM

Judas then, having received the Roman cohort and officers from the chief priests and the Pharisees, came there with lanterns and torches and weapons. So Jesus, knowing all the things that were coming upon Him, went forth and said to them, "Whom do you seek?" They answered Him, "Jesus the Nazarene." He said to them, "I am He." And Judas also, who was betraying Him, was standing with them. So when He said to them, "I am He," they drew back and fell to the ground. (18:3–6; cf. v. 8)

When Judas and the soldiers arrived to arrest Him, Jesus, the intended victim, took charge of the situation and said to them, "Whom do you seek?" They (most likely the leaders), probably stating their official orders, answered Him, "Jesus the Nazarene." The Lord said to them, "I am He." As noted in previous chapters, the word "He" is not in the original Greek. As He had done before on a number of occasions (e.g., 8:24, 28, 58), Jesus was claiming for Himself the name of God from Exodus 3:14—"I AM."

Before relating the crowd's startling response to Jesus' words, John inserts the parenthetical statement that "Judas also, who was betraying Him, was standing with them." This seemingly insignificant detail stresses yet again Jesus' absolute mastery of the circumstances. John wants to make it clear that Judas was merely one of those who experienced what was about to happen. Judas had absolutely no power over Jesus (cf. 19:11); he was jolted to the ground with the rest of those present.

Christ demonstrated His divine dominance in a stunning manner. Immediately after "He said to them, 'I am He,' they drew back and fell to the ground." All Jesus had to do was speak His name—the name of God—and His enemies were rendered helpless. This amazing demonstration of His power clearly reveals that they did not seize Jesus. He went with them willingly, to carry out the divine plan of redemption that called for His sacrificial death.

Illustrating the foolishness of unbelief, some argue that no supernatural power is in view here. Jesus' sudden appearance out of the shadows, they maintain, startled those in the front of the column. They then lurched backwards and knocked the ones behind them down, who in turn knocked others down, until the whole column went down. But the temple police and the Roman soldiers were prepared for trouble (cf. Matt. 26:55). They would surely have spread out, both to themselves against an attack by Jesus' followers, and to cut off any escape attempt on His part. The notion that hundreds of experienced police officers and highly trained soldiers would stand so close together in one long line that they could be toppled over like dominoes is ludicrous.

The Bible speaks repeatedly of the power of God's spoken word. He spoke, and the heavens and earth were created (Gen. 1:3, 6, 9, 11, 14, 20, 24, 26; cf. Ps. 33:6); Satan and mankind were judged (Gen. 3:14–19); the rebellious generation of Israelites died in the wilderness (Num. 26:65); and Israel went into exile for seventy years (2 Chron. 36:21). When the Lord Jesus Christ returns, He will execute judgment on His enemies "with the sword which [comes] from [His] mouth" (Rev. 19:21; cf. v. 15; 1:16; 2:16).

John's account highlights Christ's divine power; at His word His enemies were thrown backward to the ground. This is the power of the Great I Am, Immanuel, "God with Us." He is the King of Glory.

Appendix

———✦———

APOSTOLIC AFFIRMATIONS OF THE DEITY OF CHRIST

SELECTED SCRIPTURES

A survey of additional biblical texts demonstrates the ample testimony of the apostles to the deity of Jesus Christ. This appendix considers the witness of Thomas, Paul, the author of Hebrews, Peter, and John.

THE WITNESS OF THOMAS

After eight days His disciples were again inside, and Thomas with them. Jesus came, the doors having been shut, and stood in their midst and said, "Peace be with you." Then He said to Thomas, "Reach here with your finger, and see My hands; and reach here your hand and put it into My side; and do not be unbelieving, but believing." Thomas answered and said to Him, "My Lord and my God!" Jesus said to him, "Because you have seen Me, have you believed? Blessed are they who did not see, and yet believed." (John 20:26–29)

Not all of the apostles had been present at the appearance of the resurrected Christ recorded in John 20:19–23. Notably, Thomas was not with them when Jesus came (cf. 20:24).

After eight days the disciples were again inside, but this time Thomas was with them. Once again, the doors had been shut (cf. v. 19), and once again that proved to be no deterrent to the risen Lord. As He had done eight days earlier, Jesus came in and stood in their midst. He immediately singled out Thomas. Ever the sympathetic High Priest (Heb. 4:15). Jesus gently, lovingly, compassionately said to him, "Reach here with your finger, and see My hands; and reach here your hand and put it into My side; and do not be unbelieving, but believing."

The Lord met Thomas at the point of his weakness and doubt, without rebuke because He knew Thomas's error was connected to his profound love. In patient compassion, He gave Thomas the empirical proof he had demanded.

That was enough for Thomas; his hardened skepticism dissolved forever in light of the irrefutable evidence in the person confronting him. Overwhelmed, he made perhaps the greatest confession of any of the apostles, rivaled only by Peter's confession of Jesus as the Messiah (Matt. 16:16), exclaiming, "My Lord and my God!" Significantly, Jesus did not correct him, but accepted Thomas's affirmation of His deity. Indeed, He praised Thomas for his faith, saying to him, "Because you have seen Me, have you believed?" Then, looking ahead to the time when the tangible, physical evidence Thomas had witnessed would no longer be available, the Lord pronounced those "blessed . . . who did not see, and yet believed" (cf. 2 Cor. 5:7; 1 Peter 1:8–9).

Thomas's confession and Christ's response are a fitting lead in to John's summary statement of his goal and purpose in writing his gospel: "Therefore many other signs Jesus also performed in the presence of the disciples, which are not written in this book; but these have been written so that you may believe that Jesus is the Christ, the Son of God; and that believing you may have life in His name." To believe that Jesus Christ is God incarnate (1:1, 14), the Lamb of God who takes away the sin of the world (1:29), and the resurrection and the life (11:25) is to believe that truth that when accepted provides forgiveness of sin and eternal life (3:16).

The Witness of Paul

Romans 9:5

. . . from whom is the Christ according to the flesh, who is over all, God blessed forever. Amen.

Israel was privileged to provide the lineage of Christ according to the flesh. Christ was not incidentally born a Jew but was preordained to be a human descendant of Abraham and of David. It is for that reason that Matthew gives the genealogy of Jesus' adoptive father, Joseph (1:1–17) and that Luke gives the genealogy of His natural mother, Mary (Luke 3:23–38). Remember that Jesus Himself told the Samaritan woman that "salvation is from the Jews" and that He was the promised Jewish Messiah who would offer salvation to all mankind (John 4:22–26).

In closing this abbreviated but comprehensive account of Israel's special blessings, Paul declares that Jesus Christ—by far their greatest blessing, the blessing in whom all the others find their full meaning—"is over all, God blessed forever. Amen."

Those words are not so much a benediction as an affirmation of Christ's divine majesty and lordship. Without exception in Scripture, both in the Hebrew Old Testament and the Greek New Testament, a doxology always places the word "blessed" *before* the name of God. Here, Paul uses the reverse form, "God blessed," indicating beyond doubt that the apostle intentionally equates Christ with God. The antecedent of God is who, and the antecedent of who is Christ.

He was the supreme blessing, yet they rejected Him! Tragic unbelief that grieved the heart of Paul and grieves the heart of God Himself.

Philippians 2:5–6

. . . Christ Jesus, who, although He existed in the form of God, did not regard equality with God a thing to be grasped

In His incarnation, the Lord Jesus humbly left His heavenly throne to be born in an earthly stable, to walk among sinners, and to die on a cross for those He came to save. Jesus' humiliating step downward from His exalted position is seen in the truth that "He existed in the form of God." Before, during, and after His incarnation, He was, by His very nature, fully and eternally God. "Existed" translates a present active participle of the compound verb *huparchō,* which is formed from *hupo* ("under") and *archē* ("beginning") and denotes the continuance of a previous state or existence. It stresses the essence of a person's nature, that which is absolutely unalterable, inalienable, and unchangeable. William Barclay comments that the verb refers to "that part of a [person] which, in any circumstances, remains the same."[1]

Jesus Christ eternally and immutably existed, and will forever continue to exist, in the form of God. The word translated "form" (*morphē*) refers to the outward manifestation of an inner reality.

The idea is that, before the incarnation, from all eternity past, Jesus preexisted in the divine form of God, equal with God the Father in every way. By His very nature and innate being, Jesus Christ is, always has been, and will forever be fully divine.

The Greek word *schēma* is also often translated "form," but the meaning is quite different from that of *morphē*. As Barclay points out,

> *Morphē* is the essential form which never alters; *schēma* is the outward form which changes from time to time and from circumstance to circumstance. For instance, the essential *morphē* of any human being is humanity and this never changes; but his *schēma* is continually changing. A baby, a child, a boy, a youth, a man of middle age, an old man always have the *morphē* of humanity, but the outward *schēma* changes all the time. (*Philippians,* 35–36)[2]

"Equality with God" is synonymous with the preceding phrase "form of God." In repeating the declaration of Christ's true nature and essence, Paul emphasizes its absolute and incontestable reality. It is interesting that *isos* ("equality") is in a plural form (*isa,* "equalities"), suggesting that Paul may have been referring to every aspect of Jesus' deity. The term refers to exact equivalence. In becoming a man, Jesus did not in any way forfeit or diminish His absolute equality with God.

During His earthly ministry, Jesus never denied or minimized His deity. He was unambiguous in acknowledging His divine sonship and oneness with the Father (John 5:17–18; 10:30, 38; 14:9; 17:1, 21–22; 20:28); yet He never used His power or authority for personal advantage, because such prerogatives of His divinity were not "a thing to be grasped." He willingly suffered the worst possible humiliation rather than demand the honor, privilege, and glory that were rightly His. Nor did He use the powers of His undiminished sovereign deity to oppose the purpose of His Father because the price was too high. At any time He could have appealed to His Father and at once received "more than twelve legions of angels" to come to His defense (Matt. 26:53). But that would have thwarted His Father's plan, with which He fully concurred, and He would not do it.

Colossians 1:15

He is the image of the invisible God, the firstborn of all creation

In chapter 2 we explored this verse in detail as part of the discussion of verses 15–19 and noted that "Jesus Christ has been [the image of God] from all eternity." Jesus is firstborn in preeminence and priority, as God so describes the Messiah in Psalm 89:27, when He calls Him, "My firstborn, the highest of the kings of the earth." The rank of firstborn is not a ranking of birth order, for Jesus was neither born nor created. It is a ranking of priority. Jesus is the "name above all names."

Colossians 2:9–10

For in Him all the fullness of Deity dwells in bodily form, and in Him you have been made complete, and He is the head over all rule and authority

This is one of the most uplifting passages in all of Scripture. It presents the glorious majesty of Christ's Person and His complete sufficiency. Verse 9 is perhaps the most definitive statement of Christ's deity in the Pauline Epistles. It is the rock upon which all attempts to disprove Christ's deity are shattered. Obviously, there were heretics saying Jesus was not God, and that was the most damning and disturbing element of their false teaching—as it still is in any heretical system.

The false teaching just described was part of the satanically devised and humanly propagated religious system, and it was not according to Christ and what Scripture reveals about Him. It, like all false systems of religion, cannot save. That is the peak of its deadliness. In Christ alone "all the fullness of Deity dwells in bodily form." He alone has the power to save. The word "fullness" (*plērōma*) is the same term used in Colossians 1:19. It was a term used by the Colossian errorists. They believed the divine *plērōma* was divided in its expression among the various emanations. Each got a decreasing share as they descended the ladder from good to bad. Paul, however, insists that all the fullness of Deity, not a part of it, dwells in Christ. The verb "dwells" (*katoikeō*) means "to settle down and be at home." The present tense indicates that the essence of deity continually abides at home in Christ.

Deity is a word emphasizing divine nature. That nature of God that continually abode in Jesus Christ was not some divine light that merely lit Him up for a while, but was not His own. He is fully God forever. And as the One possessing "all the fullness of Deity," Christ is the head over all rule and authority. He was not one of a series of lesser beings emanating from God, as the false teachers maintained. Rather, He is God Himself and thus the head over all the angelic realm.

The Colossian false teachers also apparently taught a form of philosophic dualism, believing that spirit was good and matter was evil. Hence, it was unthinkable to them that God would take on a human body. Paul counters that false doctrine by emphasizing that "all the fullness of Deity dwells" in Christ in bodily form. The One who took upon Himself human nature at Bethlehem will keep that humanity for all eternity. He will forever be the God Man.

Titus 2:13

[We are] looking for the blessed hope and the appearing of the glory of our great God and Savior, Christ Jesus.

The phrase "our great God and Savior, Christ Jesus" is one of the many plain declarations in Scripture of the deity of Jesus Christ (see, for example, John 1:1–18; Rom. 9:5; Heb. 1:1–3). Some interpreters hold that in this passage "God" and "Savior" refer to different beings, the first ("great God") to the divine Father and the second ("Savior") to the human Son, Christ Jesus. But that explanation has several insurmountable problems. Besides the other clear affirmations of the divinity of Christ in Scripture are several grammatical reasons found in this passage itself. First, there is but one definite article (the, *tou*), which indicates the singularity and identity of God and Savior. Second, both of the singular pronouns in the following verse ("who," *hos*; and "Himself," *heauton*) refer back to a single person. And, although the Old Testament makes countless references to God the Father as great, in the New Testament that description is used only of God the Son (see, e.g., Matt. 5:35; Luke 1:32; 7:16; Heb. 10:21; 13:20). Perhaps most importantly, the New Testament nowhere speaks of the appearing or second coming of God the Father but only of the Son.

THE WITNESS OF THE AUTHOR OF HEBREWS

Hebrews 1:2–3

In these last days [God] has spoken to us in His Son, whom He appointed heir of all things, through whom also He made the world. And He is the radiance of His glory and the exact representation of His nature, and upholds all things by the word of His power.

When the question is brought up as to who Jesus Christ really was, some people will say He was a good teacher, some will say He was a religious fanatic, some will say He was a fake, and some will claim He was a criminal, a phantom, or a political revolutionary. Others are likely to believe that He was the highest form of humankind, who had a spark of divinity that He fanned into flame—a spark, they claim, that all of us have but seldom fan. There are countless human explanations as to who Jesus was. In these verses, we learn what God says about who Jesus was, and *is*.

"In these last days [God] has spoken to us in His Son, whom He appointed heir of all things." If Jesus is the Son of God, then He is the heir of all that God possesses. Everything that exists will find its true meaning only when it comes under the final control of Jesus Christ.

Even the Psalms predicted that He would one day be the heir to all that God possesses. "But as for Me, I have installed My King upon Zion, My holy mountain. I will surely tell of the decree of the LORD: He said to Me, 'You are My Son, today I have begotten You' " (Ps. 2:6–7). Again we read, "'Ask of Me, and I will surely give the nations as Your inheritance, and the very ends of the earth as Your possession. You shalt break them with a rod of iron, You shalt shatter them like earthenware' " (Ps. 2:8–9). And still again, "'I also shall make him My firstborn, the highest of the kings of the earth' " (Ps. 89:27). "Firstborn" does not mean that Christ did not exist before He was born as Jesus in Bethlehem. It is not primarily a chronological term at all, but has to do with legal rights—especially those of inheritance and authority. God's destined kingdom will in the last days be given finally and eternally to Jesus Christ.

Paul explains that all things not only were created by Christ but *for* Him (Col. 1:16) and that "from Him and through Him and to Him are all things. To Him be the glory forever. Amen" (Rom. 11:36). Everything that exists exists for Jesus Christ. What truth better proves His equality with God?

In his first sermon, at Pentecost, Peter told his Jewish audience, "Therefore let all the house of Israel know for certain that God has made Him both Lord and Christ—this Jesus whom you crucified" (Acts 2:36). This carpenter who died nailed to a cross is, in fact, the King of Kings and Lord of Lords. He will rule the world. Satan knew this truth when he approached Jesus in the wilderness and tempted Him to take control of the world in the wrong way, by bowing down to Satan. As the temporary usurper of God's rule over the earth, Satan continually tries every means of preventing the true Heir from receiving His inheritance.

When Christ first came to earth, He became poor for our sakes, "so that [we], through His poverty might become rich" (2 Cor. 8:9). He had nothing for Himself. He had "nowhere to lay His head" (Luke 9:58). Even His clothes were taken from Him when He died. He was buried in a grave that belonged to someone else. But when Christ comes to earth again, He will completely and eternally inherit all things. And, wonder of wonders, because we have trusted in Him, we are to be "fellow heirs with Christ" (Rom. 8:16–17).

When we enter into His eternal kingdom we will jointly possess all that He possesses. We will not be joint Christs or joint Lords, but we will be joint heirs. His marvelous inheritance will be ours as well.

The author of Hebrews continues by describing Jesus' creatorship: "through whom also He made the world." Christ is the agent through whom God created the world. "All things came into being through Him, and apart from Him nothing came into being that has come into being" (John 1:3). One of the greatest proofs of Jesus' divinity is His ability to create. Except for His complete sinlessness, His total righteousness, nothing more sets Him apart from us than His creatorship. Ability to create belongs to God alone and the fact that Jesus creates indicates that He is God. He created everything material and everything spiritual. Though man has stained His work with sin, Christ originally made it good, and the very creation itself longs to be restored to what it was in the beginning (Rom. 8:22).

The common Greek word for "world" is *kosmos*, but that is not the word used in Hebrews 1:2. The word here is *aiōnas*, which does not mean the material world but "the ages," as it is often translated. Jesus Christ is responsible not only for the physical earth; He is also responsible for creating time, space, energy, and matter. Christ created the whole universe and everything that makes it function, and He did it all without effort.

As noted in chapter 2, the vastness of our universe is staggering. The sun is 93 million miles from the earth. Our next nearest star system, Alpha Centauri, is 24 trillion miles from earth and five times larger than our sun. A ray of light travels at 186,000 miles per second, so if we could travel at that speed, it would take 2 minutes and 18 seconds to reach Venus, 4 1/2 minutes to reach Mercury, 1 hour and 11 seconds to reach Saturn, and so on. Having got that far, we would still be well inside our own solar system. To travel to Alpha Centauri, the next star system, would require 4.37 *years*. More realistically, via the US space shuttle we could reach Alpha Centauri in about 165,000 years.[3] The star Betelgeuse is 880 quadrillion miles (880 followed by fifteen zeroes) from us.

Where did it all come from? Who conceived it? Who made it? It cannot be an accident. Somebody had to make it, and the Bible tells us the Maker was Jesus Christ.

In Hebrews 1:3, the author continues by noting Christ's radiance, the brightness of the glory of God. "And He is the radiance of His glory." The term "radiance" (*apaugasma*, "to send forth light") represents Jesus as the manifestation of God. He expresses God to us. Just as the rays of the sun light and warm the earth, so Jesus Christ is the glorious light of God shining into the hearts of men. Just as the sun was never without and cannot be separated from its brightness, so God was never without and cannot be separated from the glory of Christ. Never was God without Him or He without God, and never in any way can He be separated from God. Yet the brightness of the sun is not the sun. Neither is Christ the Father in that sense. He is fully and absolutely God, yet is a distinct Person.

We would never be able to see or enjoy God's light if we did not have Jesus to look at. Standing one day before the temple, Jesus said, "I am the Light of the world; he who follows Me shall not walk in the darkness, but will have the Light of life" (John 8:12). Jesus Christ is the radiance of God's glory, and He can transmit that light into your life and my life, so that we, in turn, can radiate the glory of God. We live in a dark world. Into this dark world God sent His glorious Light. Without the Son of God, there is only darkness.

The author of Hebrews continues to describe the Lord Jesus: "And He is the radiance of His glory and the exact representation of His nature." Jesus Christ is the express image of God. Christ not only was God manifest, He was God in substance.

"Exact representation" translates the Greek term used for the impression made by a die or stamp on a seal. The design on the die is reproduced on the wax. Jesus Christ is the reproduction of God. He is the perfect, personal imprint of God in time and space. Colossians 1:15 gives a similar illustration of this incomprehensible truth: "He is the image of the invisible God." The word "image" here is *eikōn*, from which we get "icon." *Eikōn* means a precise copy, an exact reproduction, as in a fine sculpture or portrait. To call Christ the *Eikōn* of God means He is the exact reproduction of God. "For in Him all the fullness of Deity dwells in bodily form" (Col. 2:9).

Christ not only made all things and will someday inherit all things, but He also holds them all together in the meanwhile. As the biblical writer explains, He "upholds all things by the word of His power." The Greek word for upholds means "to support, to maintain," and it is used here in the present tense, implying continuous action. Everything in the universe is sustained right now by Jesus Christ.

Things do not happen in our universe by accident. They did not happen that way in the beginning. They are not going to happen that way in the end, and they are not happening that way now. Jesus Christ is sustaining the universe. He is Himself the principle of cohesion. He is not like the deist's "watchmaker" creator, who made the world, set it in motion, and has not bothered with it since. The universe is a cosmos instead of chaos, an ordered and reliable system instead of an erratic and unpredictable muddle, only because Jesus Christ upholds it.

When I think about Christ's power to uphold the universe,

that truth goes right to my heart. When Christ "[begins a good work in you" (Phil. 1:6), He holds onto it and sustains it all the way through, just as He continues to sustains the universe. We can imagine Jude's excitement when he wrote, "Now to Him who is able to keep you from stumbling, and to make you stand in the presence of His glory blameless with great joy, to the only God our Savior, through Jesus Christ our Lord, be glory, majesty, dominion and authority, before all time and now and forever. Amen" (Jude 24–25). When your life is given to Jesus Christ, He holds it and sustains it and one day will take it into God's very presence. A life, just as a universe, that is not sustained by Christ is chaos.

Hebrews 1:8

But of the Son He says, "Your throne, O God, is forever and ever, And the righteous scepter is the scepter of His kingdom."

Here is one of the most amazing and important statements in all of Scripture: Jesus is God eternal! This verse expands on the difference between Christ's nature and that of angels. Those who say Jesus was just a man, or just one of many angels, or one of many prophets of God, or was but a subgod of some sort are lying and bringing upon themselves the anathema, the curse, of God. Jesus is no less than God. The Father says to the Son, "Your throne, O God, is forever and ever." God the Father acknowledges God the Son. This verse gives one of the most powerful, emphatic, and irrefutable proofs of the deity of Christ in the Bible—from the Father Himself.

The Father's testimony about the Son corresponds to the Son's testimony about Himself. Throughout His ministry Jesus claimed equality with God. "For this reason therefore the Jews were seeking all the more to kill Him, because He not only was breaking the Sabbath, but also was calling God His own Father, making Himself equal with God" (John 5:18). When He said, "I and the Father are one" (John 10:30), the Jewish leaders well understood His claim. In light of who they thought He was, a mere man, their reaction was to be expected. "For a good work we do not stone You, but for blasphemy; and because You, being a man, make Yourself out to be God" (v. 33).

Talking about Israel and all their blessings, Paul wrote, "whose are the fathers, and from whom is the Christ according to the flesh, who is over all, God blessed forever. Amen" (Rom. 9:5). The Greek text more accurately reads, "God who is over all, blessed forever." The claim is that Jesus Christ is God. In 1 Timothy 3:16 the same apostle writes, "And by common confession great is the mystery of godliness: He who was revealed in the flesh, was vindicated in the Spirit, seen by angels, proclaimed among the nations, believed on in the world, taken up in glory." Still again Paul declares that believers are "looking for the blessed hope and the appearing of the glory of our great God and Savior, Christ Jesus" (Titus 2:13).

In his first letter, John says, "And we know that the Son of God has come, and has given us understanding so that we may know Him who is true; and we are in Him who is true, in His Son Jesus Christ. This is the true God and eternal life" (1 John 5:20). Throughout the New Testament the claim is unequivocal: Jesus Christ is God.

In Hebrews 1:8 we continue reading, "Your throne, O God, is forever and ever, and the righteous scepter is the scepter of His kingdom." Jesus Christ has an eternal throne, from which He rules eternity as God and King. He is the eternal King, with an eternal kingdom, and an eternal scepter of righteousness.

The Witness of Peter

Simon Peter, a bond-servant and apostle of Jesus Christ, to those who have received a faith of the same kind as ours, by the righteousness of our God and Savior, Jesus Christ. (2 Peter 1:1)

Believers' saving faith is available because of the righteousness of Jesus Christ. Sinners are given eternal life because the Savior imputes His perfect righteousness to them (2 Cor. 5:21; Phil. 3:8–9; 1 Peter 2:24), covering their sins and rendering them acceptable to Him. Romans 4:4–8 says,

> Now to the one who works, his wage is not credited as a favor, but as what is due. But to the one who does not work, but believes in Him who justifies the ungodly, his faith is credited as righteousness, just as David also speaks of the blessing on the man to whom God credits righteousness apart from works: "Blessed are those whose lawless deeds have been forgiven, and whose sins have been covered. Blessed is the man whose sin the Lord will not take into account."

This immensely important doctrine of imputed righteousness is at the very heart of the Christian gospel. Salvation is a gift from God at all points. Both the faith to believe and the righteousness to satisfy God's holiness come from Him. On the cross Christ bore the full wrath of God against all the sins of those who would believe (2 Cor. 5:18–19). Those sins were imputed to Christ so that God could impute to believers all the righteousness that was His. His righteousness fully covers the redeemed, as the prophet Isaiah beautifully expresses it, "I will rejoice greatly in the Lord, my soul will exult in my God; for He has clothed me with garments of salvation, He has wrapped me with a robe of righteousness, as a bridegroom decks himself with a garland, and as a bride adorns herself with her jewels" (Isa. 61:10).

It is noteworthy that Peter does not refer to God our Father here but to "our God and Savior, Jesus Christ." Righteousness here does not proceed from the Father, but it reaches every believer through the Son, Jesus Christ (cf. Gal. 3:8–11; Phil. 3:8–9). The Greek construction places just one article before the phrase "God and Savior," which makes both terms refer to the same person. Thus Peter identifies Jesus, not just as Savior, but as God (cf. 1:11; 2:20; 3:2, 18; Isa. 43:3, 11; 45:15, 21; 60:16; Rom. 9:5; Col. 2:9; Titus 2:13; Heb. 1:8), the author and agent of salvation. The apostle made the same relation clear in his Pentecost sermon, in which he took the Old Testament truth of God and applied it to Jesus (Acts 2:21–36; cf. Matt. 1:21; Acts 4:12; 5:31).

The Witness of John

1 John 5:20–21

And we know that the Son of God has come, and has given us understanding so that we may know Him who is true; and we are in Him who is true, in His Son Jesus Christ. This is the true God and eternal life. Little children, guard yourselves from idols.

These closing verses bring John's first epistle full circle. John began with the coming of the Word of Life (1:1–4); now he closes with the certainty that "the Son of God has come. The present tense of the verb "come" (*hēkō*) indicates that Jesus has come and is still present. The Christian faith is not theoretical or abstract; it is rooted in the practical truth that God became man in the Person of Jesus Christ.

THE DEITY OF CHRIST

Because no one can know "who the Father is except the Son, and anyone to whom the Son wills to reveal Him" (Luke 10:22), Jesus "has given us understanding so that we may know Him who is true" (1 John 5:20). But beyond mere knowledge, Christians have a personal union "with Him who is true, in His Son Jesus Christ" (cf. Rom. 8:1; 1 Cor. 1:30; 2 Cor. 5:17; 1 Peter 5:14). The Bible teaches that the only way to know the true and living God is through Jesus Christ. No one can be saved who does not believe in Christ, for there is no salvation apart from Him (cf. 2:1–2; 4:10, 14; 5:1; John 14:6; Acts 4:12).

John's threefold use of the word "true" (*alēthinos*) in this verse stresses the importance of understanding the truth in a world filled with Satan's lies. The last use of the term points to the most significant truth of all—that Jesus Christ "is the true God and eternal life." The deity of Jesus Christ is an essential element of the Christian faith, and no one who rejects it can be saved.

Revelation 1:17–18

When I saw Him, I fell at His feet like a dead man. And He placed His right hand on me, saying, "Do not be afraid; I am the first and the last, and the living One; and I was dead, and behold, I am alive forevermore, and I have the keys of death and of Hades."

In a manner similar to his experience with the glory of Jesus on the Mount of Transfiguration more than six decades earlier (cf. Matt. 17:6), John was again overwhelmed with terror at the manifestation of Christ's glory and "fell at His feet like a dead man." Such fear was standard for those few who experienced such unusual heavenly visions. When an angel appeared to him, Daniel reported that "no strength was left in me, for my natural color turned to a deathly pallor, and I retained no strength. . . . and as soon as I heard the sound of his words, I fell into a deep sleep on my face, with my face to the ground" (Dan. 10:8–9; cf. 8:17). Overwhelmed by the vision of God that he saw in the temple, Isaiah cried out, "Woe is me, for I am ruined! Because I am a man of unclean lips, and I live among a people of unclean lips; for my eyes have seen the King, the LORD of hosts" (Isa. 6:5). Ezekiel saw several visions of the Lord's glory and his response was always the same: he fell on his face (Ezek. 1:28; 3:23; 9:8; 43:3; 44:4). After the Angel of the Lord appeared to them and announced the birth of Samson, "Manoah [Samson's father] said to his wife, 'We shall surely die, for we have seen God' " (Judg. 13:22). Job had a similar reaction after God spoke to him: "I have heard of You by the hearing of the ear; but now my eye sees You; therefore I retract, and I repent in dust and ashes" (Job 42:5–6).

The New Testament records two instances of those who fell before the glory of the Almighty, one in the past as well as multitudes in the future. On his way to Damascus to persecute Christians, Saul of Tarsus (better known as the apostle Paul) "saw on the way a light from heaven, brighter than the sun, shining all around me and those who were journeying with me" (Acts 26:13). In response, Saul and his companions fell prostrate in the road (v. 14). After witnessing the terrifying calamities that follow the opening of the sixth seal, unbelievers during the tribulation to come will cry out in terror "to the mountains and to the rocks, 'Fall on us and hide us from the presence of Him who sits on the throne, and from the wrath of the Lamb; for the great day of their wrath has come, and who is able to stand?' " (Rev. 6:16–17).

In stark contrast to the silly, false, and boastful claims of many in our own day who claim to have seen God, the reaction of those in Scripture who genuinely saw God was inevitably one of fear. Those brought face-to-face with the blazing, holy glory of the Lord Jesus Christ were terrified, realizing their sinful unworthiness to be in His holy presence. Summarizing the proper response to God's holiness and majesty, the writer of Hebrews exhorts believers to "offer to God an acceptable service with reverence and awe; for our God is a consuming fire" (Heb. 12:28–29).

As He had done so long ago at the transfiguration (Matt. 17:7), Jesus placed His right hand on John and comforted him. This is a touch of comfort and reassurance. There is comfort for Christians overwhelmed by the glory and majesty of Christ in the assurance of His gracious love and merciful forgiveness. Jesus' comforting words, "Do not be afraid," (lit. "Stop being afraid") reveal His compassionate assurance of the terrified apostle. Similar words of comfort are God's response throughout Scripture to those overwhelmed by His majestic presence (e.g., Gen. 15:1; 26:24; Judg. 6:23; Matt. 14:27; 17:7; 28:10).

The comfort Jesus offered was based on who He is and the authority He possesses. First, He identified Himself as "I Am" (*egō eimi*)—the covenant name of God (cf. Ex. 3:14). It was that name with which He had comforted the terrified disciples who saw Him walking on the Sea of Galilee (Matt. 14:27). Jesus took that name for Himself in John 8:58—a direct claim to deity that was not lost on His opponents (v. 59).

Jesus next identified Himself as "the first and the last" (cf. 2:8; 22:13), a title used of God in the Old Testament (Isa. 44:6; 48:12; cf. 41:4). When all false gods have come and gone, only He remains. He existed before them and will continue to exist eternally, long after they have been forgotten. Jesus' application of that title to Himself is another powerful proof of His deity.

The third title of deity Jesus claimed is that of "the living One" (cf. John 1:4; 14:6). That also is a title used throughout Scripture to describe God (e.g., Josh. 3:10; 1 Sam. 17:26; Ps. 84:2; Hos. 1:10; Matt. 16:16; 26:63; Acts 14:15; Rom. 9:26; 2 Cor. 3:3; 6:16; 1 Thess. 1:9; 1 Tim. 3:15; 4:10; Heb. 3:12; 9:14; 10:31; Rev. 7:2). God is the eternal, uncaused, self-existent One. In John 5:26 Jesus said to His Jewish opponents, "Just as the Father has life in Himself, even so He gave to the Son also to have life in Himself," thus claiming full equality with God the Father.

The One whose presence struck fear into John's heart, the I Am, the first and the last, the living One, the One whose death freed him from his sins (Rev. 1:5) is the very One who comforted and reassured John. In the words of the apostle Paul, "What then shall we say to these things? If God is for us, who is against us?" (Rom. 8:31).

Christ's seemingly paradoxical declaration "I was dead, and behold, I am alive forevermore" provides further grounds for assurance. The Greek text literally reads, "I became dead." The living One, the eternal, self-existent God who could never die, became man and died. As Peter explains in 1 Peter 3:18, Christ was "put to death in the flesh, but made alive in the spirit." In His humanness He died without ceasing to live as God.

"Behold" introduces a statement of amazement and wonder: "I am alive forevermore." Christ lives forever in a union of glorified humanity and deity, "according to the power of an indestructible life" (Heb. 7:16). "Christ, having been raised from the dead," wrote Paul, "is never to die again; death no longer is master over Him" (Rom. 6:9). That truth provides comfort and assurance, because Jesus "is able also to save forever those who draw near to God through Him, since He always lives to make intercession for them" (Heb. 7:25). In spite of his sinfulness in the presence of the glorious

Lord of heaven, John had nothing to fear because that same Lord had paid by His death the penalty for John's sins (and those of all who believe in Him) and risen to be his eternal advocate.

As the eternal I Am, the first and the last, the living One, Jesus holds "the keys of death and of Hades." Those terms are essentially synonymous, with death being the condition and Hades the place. Hades is the New Testament equivalent of the Old Testament term Sheol and refers to the place of the dead. Keys denote access and authority. Jesus Christ has the authority to decide who dies and who lives; He controls life and death. And John, like all the redeemed, had nothing to fear, since Christ had already delivered him from death and Hades by His own death.

Knowing that Christ has authority over death provides assurance, since believers need no longer fear it. Jesus declared, "I am the resurrection and the life; he who believes in Me will live even if he dies. . . . because I live, you will live also." (John 11:25; 14:19). To die, Paul noted, is "to be absent from the body and to be at home with the Lord" (2 Cor. 5:8; cf. Phil. 1:23). Jesus conquered Satan and took the keys of death away from him: "Through death [Christ rendered] powerless him who had the power of death, that is, the devil, and . . . free[d] those who through fear of death were subject to slavery all their lives" (Heb. 2:14–15). The knowledge that Christ "loves us and released us from our sins by His blood" (Rev. 1:5) provides the assurance that is the balance to the reverential fear that His glory and majesty evoke.

Revelation 19:11–13

And I saw heaven opened, and behold, a white horse, and He who sat on it is called Faithful and True, and in righteousness He judges and wages war. His eyes are a flame of fire, and on

His head are many diadems; and He has a name written on Him which no one knows except Himself. He is clothed with a robe dipped in blood, and His name is called The Word of God.

The time has come at last for the full, glorious revelation of the sovereign Lord. This is the time to which all of Revelation (as well as all of redemptive history) has been pointing, the time of which Jesus Himself spoke in Matthew 24:27–31.

As the dramatic scene unfolds, John stands transfixed, his attention riveted on the majestic, regal, mighty Rider. Jesus, the One who ascended to heaven (Acts 1:9–11) where He has been seated at the Father's right hand (Acts 5:31; 7:55–56; Rom. 8:34; Eph. 1:20; Col. 3:1; Heb. 1:3, 13; 8:1; 10:12; 12:2; 1 Peter 3:22), is about to receive the kingdom that the Father promised Him. In an earlier vision, John saw Jesus receive the title deed to the earth:

> I saw in the right hand of Him who sat on the throne a book written inside and on the back, sealed up with seven seals. And I saw a strong angel proclaiming with a loud voice, "Who is worthy to open the book and to break its seals?" And no one in heaven or on the earth or under the earth was able to open the book or to look into it. Then I began to weep greatly because no one was found worthy to open the book or to look into it; and one of the elders said to me, "Stop weeping; behold, the Lion that is from the tribe of Judah, the Root of David, has overcome so as to open the book and its seven seals."
>
> And I saw between the throne (with the four living creatures) and the elders a Lamb standing, as if slain, having seven horns and seven eyes, which are the seven Spirits of God, sent out into all the earth. And He came and took the book out of the right hand of Him who sat on the throne. (5:1–7)

The Lamb of that vision has become the conquering King.

No longer is Jesus portrayed as He was in His humiliation, "humble, and mounted on a donkey, even on a colt, the foal of a donkey" (Zech. 9:9). Instead, He rides the traditional white horse ridden by victorious Roman generals in their triumphal processions through the streets of Rome. White also symbolizes the spotless, unblemished, absolutely holy character of the Rider. The horse, like the crowns (v. 12), the sharp sword (v. 15), the rod of iron (v. 15), and the wine press (v. 15) is symbolic; Christ's coming is reality. The symbolic language represents various aspects of that reality—Christ's victory over His enemies, His sovereign rule, and His judgment of sinners.

Continuing his description of the astonishing scene before him, John notes that He who sat on the white horse "is called Faithful and True." There is no more appropriate name for the Lord Jesus Christ, who earlier in Revelation was called "the faithful and true Witness" (3:14). He is faithful to His promises (cf. 2 Cor. 1:20) and what He speaks is always true (John 8:45–46; Titus 1:2). Though some would like to pick and choose which teachings of Jesus they wish to accept, He is just as faithful to His promises of wrath and judgment as He is to His promises of grace and salvation. The description of Jesus as Faithful and True is in marked contrast with the unfaithfulness and lies of Satan (12:9), Antichrist's evil empire (18:23), and wicked people (2 Tim. 3:13). The very fact that He is coming again as He promised confirms that Jesus is Faithful and True.

Because Jesus is faithful to His word and righteous character, it follows that in righteousness He judges. His holy nature demands a holy, righteous reaction to sin. And because He always does what He says, He must judge the wicked (Matt. 16:27; 25:31–46; John 5:22, 27; cf. Acts 10:42; 17:31; Rom. 2:16; 2 Thess. 1:7–9; 2 Tim.

4:1). Jesus came the first time as Savior; He will return as Judge. When He came the first time, wicked people, including Pilate, Herod, Annas, and Caiaphas judged Him; when He returns, He will judge all wicked people (Acts 17:31). And He will not only be their judge, but also their executioner (vv. 15, 21). Angels may gather the wicked for judgment (Matt. 13:41), but the Lord Jesus will pass sentence on them.

No longer the Suffering Servant of His incarnation, the Lord Jesus Christ is seen in this vision as the warrior King who wages war against His foes. He is the executioner of all ungodly, unbelieving sinners. The only other reference in Scripture to Jesus waging war is in 2:16, when He warned the worldly church at Pergamum, "Repent; or else I am coming to you quickly, and I will make war against them with the sword of My mouth." This is not out of keeping with God's character, however. After their deliverance from the Egyptian forces at the Red Sea, Israel sang, "The Lord is a warrior" (Ex. 15:3; cf. Pss. 24:8; 45:3–5).

Jesus' adversaries this time will be the hardened sinners who have defied His judgments and scorned the gospel message during the Tribulation. Despite all the devastating judgments they will have experienced, and the powerful gospel preaching they will have heard, they will stubbornly refuse to repent (9:20–21; 16:9, 11). Since neither judgment nor preaching moves them to repent, Jesus will return to destroy them and send them to hell.

Unlike other conquerors the world has seen, covetousness, ambition, pride, or power will not motivate this Conqueror. He will come in utter righteousness, in perfect holiness, and in strict accord with every holy interest. Heaven cannot be at peace with sin, for God's "eyes are too pure to approve evil, and [He] cannot look on wickedness with favor" (Hab. 1:13). There is a limit to God's patience. Justice cannot always tolerate injustice; truth cannot forever tolerate lies; rebellion cannot be permitted to go on forever. Incorrigible, incurable, hardened sinners will face destruction; mercy abused and grace rejected will ultimately bring judgment.

Describing the personal appearance of the majestic, awe-inspiring Rider, John writes that "His eyes are a flame of fire." Nothing escapes the notice of His penetrating, piercing vision. He can see into the deepest recesses of the human heart, because "all things are open and laid bare to the eyes of Him with whom we have to do" (Heb. 4:13). Those eyes had reflected tenderness and joy as He gathered little children to Himself. They had reflected compassion when He observed distressed and dispirited people, wandering aimlessly through life like sheep without a shepherd. And they had reflected forgiveness when He restored Peter, who had been crushed by guilt over his shocking denial of his Master. The eyes that wept over the fate of unrepentant Jerusalem and over the sorrow, suffering, and death in this sin-cursed world, John sees flashing with the fire of judgment.

On His head John noted that Christ wore many diadems, a transliteration of the Greek word *diadēma,* which refers to a ruler's crown (cf. 12:3; 13:1). In this case, they are worn by Jesus to signify His royal rank and regal authority. Christ alone will be sovereign, since He alone is "King of Kings, and Lord of Lords" (v. 16), and "the kingdom of the world has become the kingdom of our Lord and of His Christ; and He will reign forever and ever" (11:15). The many crowns Christ will wear are indeed a fair exchange for a crown of thorns (cf. Phil. 2:8–11).

Further, John notes that Jesus had "a name written on Him which no one knows except Himself." All speculation as to the meaning of that name is obviously pointless, since the text plainly states that no one knows it except Jesus Himself. Even the inspired apostle John could not comprehend it. Maybe it will be made known after His return.

Describing the final element of Christ's appearance, John writes that "He is clothed with a robe dipped in blood." The blood is not representative of that which He shed on the cross; this is a picture of judgment, not redemption. That the Rider's name is called The Word of God identifies Him unmistakably as the Lord Jesus Christ (John 1:1, 14; 1 John 1:1). The second Person of the Trinity, the incarnate Son of God is called The Word of God because He is the revelation of God. He is the full expression of the mind, will, and purpose of God, "the radiance of His glory and the exact representation of His nature" (Heb. 1:3).

The Lord Jesus Christ will not return alone, but will be accompanied by the armies which are in heaven (cf. 17:14). Four divisions make up these glorified troops. Earlier in chapter 19 the bride of the Lamb (the church) was pictured wearing fine linen, white and clean (vv. 7–8). Those glorified believers will accompany Christ. So will the Tribulation believers, who are also pictured in heaven wearing white robes (7:9). The third group is the Old Testament saints, who are resurrected at the end of the Tribulation (Dan. 12:1–2). Finally, the holy angels will also accompany Christ (Matt. 25:31). The white horses ridden by the heavenly cavalry are not literal horses, any more than those ridden by hell's cavalry in 9:7 and 16. Unlike the Lord Jesus Christ, the heavenly army is unarmed; He alone will destroy His enemies. The saints will come not to fight with Jesus, but to reign with Him (20:4–6; 1 Cor. 6:2).

The rule of the King is described in graphic, powerful imagery. John notes first that "from His mouth comes a sharp sword." The apostle had seen that sword in an earlier vision (1:16), where it was used to defend the church against the onslaught of Satan's forces. Here it is the sword of judgment, the flaming sword dealing death to the King's foes. That the sword comes out of His mouth symbolizes the deadly power of Christ's words. Once He spoke words of comfort, but now He speaks words of death.

Christ will wield that sword with deadly effect as He strikes down the nations. His elect, both from the Gentile nations and from Israel, will be preserved; the wicked He will slaughter instantly. The dead will include all those gathered for battle at Armageddon; none will escape. The rest of the world's unredeemed people will be judged and executed at the sheep and goat judgment (Matt. 25:31–46) that follows Christ's return. This is the final stroke of death in the Day of the Lord.[4]

The stern, swift judgment that marks the onset of Christ's kingdom will be the pattern of His rule throughout the millennium. During His thousand-year reign, He will rule the nations with a rod of iron (cf. 12:5; Ps. 2:8–9); He will swiftly judge all sin and instantly put down any rebellion. All people will be required to conform to His law or face immediate judgment. In a final look at the returning King, John saw in his vision that Christ wore a banner around His robe and on His thigh (across His chest and hanging down on His upper leg as He rides), on which "He has a name written, 'King of Kings, and Lord of Lords'" (Rev. 19:16; cf. 17:14; Deut. 10:17; 1 Tim. 6:15). This is the third name given to the Lord Jesus Christ in this passage. The incomprehensible name of verse 12 may express the mystery of His essential deity. Verse 13 calls Him the Word of God, expressing His incarnation as the Son of God. The name "King of Kings, and Lord of Lords" expresses His sovereign triumph over all foes and His absolute rule in His soon-to-be-established kingdom.

NOTES

Chapter 1: The Eternal Glory of the Divine Word

1. Marcus Dods, "John" in W. Robertson Nicoll, ed. *The Expositors' Bible Commentary* (Reprint; Peabody, Mass.: Hendrickson, 2002), 1:683. Emphasis in original.

2. Specifically, see Jeremiah 1:2; Ezekiel 1:3; Daniel 9:2; Hosea 1:1; Joel 1:1; Jonah 1:1; Micah 1:1; Zephaniah 1:1; Haggai 1:1; Zechariah 1:1; Malachi 1:1.

3. W. Robert Cook, *The Theology of John* (Chicago: Moody, 1979), 49.

4. Charles Wesley, "And Can It Be?", verse 3 and refrain *Worship and Service Hymnal* (Chicago: Hope, 1957), 259.

5. Cf. H. E. Dana and Julius R. Mantey, *A Manual Grammar of the Greek New Testament* (Toronto: MacMillan, 1957), 139–40; A. T. Robertson, *The Minister and His Greek New Testament* (Grand Rapids: Baker, 1978), 67–68.

6. Robert L. Reymond *Jesus, Divine Messiah* (Philipsburg, N.J.: Presb. & Ref., 1990), 303.

7. Leon Morris, *The Gospel According to John,* The New International Commentary on the New Testament (Grand Rapids: Eerdmans, 1979], 77 n. 15.

8. H. A. W. Meyer, *Critical and Exegetical Hand-Book to the Gospel of John* (Reprint; Winona Lake, Ind.: Alpha, 1979), 48.

Chapter 2: The Glorious Preeminence of Jesus Christ

1. Donald B. DeYoung, "Design in Nature: The Anthropic Principle," *Impact*, no. 149 (November 1985): ii.

2. As cited in DeYoung, "Design in Nature," iii.

3. D. Lee Chesnut, *The Atom Speaks*, (San Diego: Creation Science Research Center, 1973), 31–33.

4. Quoted in ibid., 38.

5. Ibid.

6. J. B. Lightfoot, *St. Paul's Epistles to the Colossians and to Philemon* (1879; reprint, Grand Rapids: Zondervan, 1959), 102.

7. John Owen, *The Glory of Christ* (Reprint, Chicago: Moody, 1949), 25–26.

Chapter 5: Christ's Authority over the Sabbath

1. For a complete harmony of the Gospels, see John MacArthur, *One Perfect Life* (Nashville: Nelson, 2012).

2. For a more detailed discussion of the rabbinic Sabbath restrictions, see Alfred Edersheim, "The Ordinances and Law of the Sabbath as Laid Down in the Mishnah and the Jerusalem Talmud," Appendix XVII in *The Life and Times of Jesus the Messiah* (Grand Rapids: Eerdmans, 1974), 2:777–87.

Chapter 8: Equal with God

1. F. F. Bruce, *New Testament History* (New York: Doubleday, 1971), 165.

2. J. Gresham Machen, *Christianity and Liberalism* (1923; reprint; Grand Rapids: Eerdmans, 1974), 85.

3. Jesus referred to the kingdom as the kingdom of God in Matt. 12:28; 19:24; 21:31; Mark 1:15; Luke 4:43; and John 3:3. He identified God's kingdom as His kingdom in Matt. 13:41; 16:28; cf. Luke 1:33; 2 Tim. 4:1.

4. Compare F. F. Bruce, *The New Testament Documents: Are They Reliable?* (Downers Grove, Ill.: InterVarsity, 1973).

5. William Lane Craig, *Apologetics: An Introduction* (Chicago: Moody, 1984), 160.

6. For a discussion of the New Testament believer's relationship to the Old Testament Sabbath see John MacArthur, *Colossians and Philemon*, The MacArthur New Testament Commentary Series (Chicago: Moody Press, 1992), 118–19.

7. D. A. Carson, *The Gospel According to John,* The Pillar New Testament Commentary (Grand Rapids: Eerdmans, 1991), 255.

8. John Heading, *What the Bible Teaches: John* (Kilmarnock, Scotland: John Ritchie, 1988), 93.

Chapter 9: One with the Father

1. See John 1: 10–11; 2:20; 3:32; 4:1–3; 5:16–18; 6:41–43, 66; 7:1, 20, 26–27, 30–52; 8:13–59; 9:16, 24, 29, 40–41; 10:20; 11:46–57; 12:37–40.

2. Gerald L. Borchert, *John 1–11,* The New American Commentary (Nashville: Broadman & Holman, 2002), 337–38.

3. Leon Morris, *Reflections on the Gospel of John* (Peabody, Mass.: Hendrickson, 2000), 396.

Chapter 10: The Great I AM

1. Charles Spurgeon, "Rightly Dividing the Word of Truth," in *The Metropolitan Tabernacle Pulpit*, vol. 21 (Pasadena, Tex.: Pilgrim, 1980), 88.

2. Cited in F. F. Bruce, *The Gospel of John* (Grand Rapids: Eerdmans, 1983), 206, n. 1.

3. Leon Morris, *The Gospel According to John,* The New International Commentary on the New Testament (Grand Rapids: Eerdmans, 1979), 438.

4. R. C. H. Lenski, *The Interpretation of St. John's Gospel* (Reprint; Peabody, Mass.: Hendrickson, 1998), 614.

5. Homer Kent, *Light in the Darkness* (Grand Rapids: Baker, 1974), 128–29.

6. The Greek preposition *huper* refers to Christ's substitutionary atonement in eight of Paul's letters: Romans 5:6, 8; 8:32; 1 Corinthians 11:24; 15:3; 2 Corinthians 5:14, 15, 21; Galatians. 1:4; 2:20; 3:13; Ephesians 5:2, 25; 1 Thessalonians 5:9–10; 1 Timothy 2:6; and Titus 2:14.

7. Lenski, *The Interpretation of St. John's Gospel*, 803.

8. F. F. Bruce, *The Gospel of John* (Grand Rapids: Eerdmans, 1983), 298.

Appendix: Apostolic Affirmations of the Deity of Christ

1. William Barclay, *The Letters to the Philippians, Colossians, and Thessalonians,* rev. ed. (Louisville: Westminster, 1975), 35.

2. Ibid., 35–36.

3. Samantha Mathewson, "Proxima by the Numbers: Possibly Earth-Like World at the Next Star Over," August 24, 2016; www.space.com/33837-earth-like-planet-proxima-centauri-numbers.html.

4. On "day of the Lord" cf. Isaiah 66:15–16; Ezekiel 39:1–4, 17–20; Joel 3:12–21; Matthew 25:31–46; and 2 Thessalonians 1:6–9; 2:8.

ACKNOWLEDGMENTS

Our thanks to Nathan Busenitz in gathering and organizing material from various books in the thirty-three volume MacArthur New Testament Bible Commentary for this book in the John MacArthur Study Series. Nathan also added brief introductions to the final chapter and the appendix.

Our special thanks to the team at Moody Publishers, particularly senior editor Jim Vincent and acquiring editor Drew Dyck. Jim updated sources and examples and tightened the text in key places; Drew had valuable suggestions throughout.

PULPIT OF **JOHN CALVIN** | ST. PIERRE CATHEDRAL | GENEVA, SWITZERLAND

WE PREACH **CHRIST**

THE MASTER'S SEMINARY

13248 Roscoe Boulevard, Los Angeles, California 91352
1.800.CALL.TMS   TMS.EDU

> "*Fundamentals of the Faith* is the outgrowth of the belief that the essence of Christianity is truth—the truth about God, the truth about man, and the truth about Christ."
> **—John MacArthur**

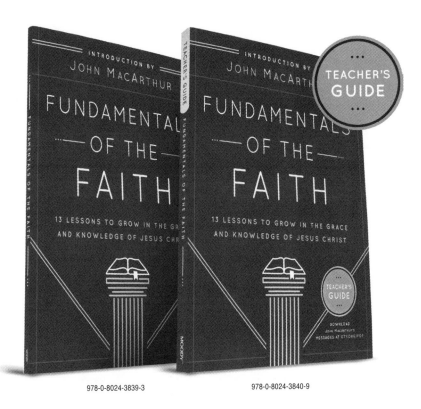

978-0-8024-3839-3   978-0-8024-3840-9

Fundamentals of the Faith is a rich and easy-to-follow workbook, developed through decades of refinement by elders, teachers, and pastors at Grace Community Church. Under the leadership of John MacArthur, this foundational material has been taught and tested in the classroom and has proven effective through the lives it has changed.

Also available in Spanish and as eBooks.

MOODY Publishers®